"As usual, Phil Ryken hides his deep scholarship behind readable prose. But the footnotes reveal that he draws on some of the most penetrating scholarly treatments of St. Paul's text. He combines all that with pastoral experience and insight. The result is a masterful, accessible exposition of this great chapter."

Tim Keller, Pastor, Redeemer Presbyterian Church, New York City; bestselling author, *The Reason for God*

"It would be hard to think of a single topic more talked about, sung about, and celebrated than love. Yet—partly because of its familiarity—love is typically taken for granted and often misconstrued by the very people who talk about it most. And let's face it: that is true even in the church. We are indebted to Phil Ryken for this wonderfully fresh, biblical analysis of what genuine love is like when we see it in perfect Christ-like purity. At once both simple and profound, this book will almost certainly challenge your presuppositions about love and help you see authentic love in a whole new light."

John MacArthur, Pastor-Teacher, Grace Community Church, Sun Valley, California

"Through his unique design for this book, Ryken explicates Paul's Love Chapter through snapshots of Jesus and the disciples. He thereby immerses us in the luxuriant love of Jesus and heartens us to pass it on. Let this book envelop you altogether in the fullness of the triune God's exuberant love!"

Marva J. Dawn, Teaching Fellow in Spiritual Theology, Regent College; author, *Truly the Community*

"Phil Ryken is not only a scholar; he is a magnificent expositor of God's Word. We already benefit from his massive commentaries on so many books of the Bible, and now he turns his attention, both as scholar and as pastor, to the message of 1 Corinthians 13. This is a gift to the entire church."

R. Albert Mohler Jr., President, The Southern Baptist Theological Seminary

"So much of following Jesus is a matter of being reminded of what we once knew. I knew that he loved me first and that his loving lay at the heart of my small ability to love others. I knew once that when my love ran out, his remained and would refill to overflowing. I knew these things, but had largely forgotten them. I will always be grateful to Phil Ryken for this profound reminder."

Michael Card, musician; Bible teacher; author, *A Better Freedom*

"Jesus said, 'By this all people will know that you are my disciples, if you have love for one another.' But what does it mean to love others? By looking at the love of Jesus in the light of 1 Corinthians 13, Phil Ryken gives us the biblical answer. *Loving the Way Jesus Loves* is surely one of the most heart-searching books I have ever read. This book is a must read for all who want to grow in Christian love."

Jerry Bridges, author, *The Pursuit of Holiness*

"Based on careful study, steeped in Scripture, and very aware of the world we live in and of the experiences people go through, Ryken shows how we can love with the kind of love that God demonstrated to us. These qualities have made Ryken a favorite author of mine and of my wife."

Ajith Fernando, Teaching Directc

"Phil Ryken majors on what is truly major when he focuses on the central attribute that is supposed to distinguish those who follow Jesus—that we love one another. And the definition of love he sets forth doesn't float abstractly in thin air but is solidly embodied by Jesus himself. I can't think of a more timely book than this one or a message the church needs more desperately than the call to love as Jesus loved. Phil has done us all a favor by shepherding us to pursue the centerpiece of our call to be like Jesus."

Carolyn Custis James, President, Synergy Women's Network; author, *When Life and Beliefs Collide*

"Another outstanding contribution by Phil Ryken that challenges me to the core of my being as a follower of Christ. If indeed it is all about love—God's love for a lost and hurting world—then the question is, as a Christ follower, how well am I imitating that love? This insightful look at the Love Chapter will make us think again if we dare to think, I am loving like Christ."

Emery Lindsay, Senior Bishop, Chairman of the Board, Church of Christ (Holiness) USA

"There are many expositions of 1 Corinthians 13, but few show how God's love in Christ Jesus is the very best exposition and truest embodiment of love. Unpacking the Love Chapter through this prism, Ryken lends great clarity to Paul's meditation on love and shows how such love drives us back to renewed adoration of Christ. Reflecting on how Christ, by his life and death, makes 1 Corinthians 13 leap from the page, drives home the frequent lovelessness of our own lives, strips bare all notions of love that are little more than sentimental twaddle, and provides a concrete robustness to love that is part and parcel of trusting and following Christ."

D. A. Carson, Research Professor of New Testament, Trinity Evangelical Divinity School

"*Loving the Way Jesus Loves* is deeply instructive of the nature of true Christian love, the extent of Jesus's own expressions of that love, and the ways in which we, his followers, are to show forth his love from our lives. This study honors Christ in two ways: by putting him on display as the great lover that he is, and by calling us to emulate our Lord in living increasingly the life of love that he expressed. Meditation on the love of Christ and on loving like Jesus—that's what this book encourages with great insight and depth."

Bruce Ware, Professor of Christian Theology, The Southern Baptist Theological Seminary

"God's unconditional love blows up all our conditional categories. It's untamable and promiscuous. It comes our way minus our merit. It's vertical one-wayness, though, compels horizontal expression. Love from God inevitably shows itself in love for others. And this is what Phil Ryken demonstrates so well. Writing as a pastor-scholar, Ryken makes a passionate plea for the church to rediscover what Francis Schaeffer called 'the final apologetic'—namely, love. It's what matters most."

Tullian Tchividjian, Pastor, Coral Ridge Presbyterian Church; author, *Jesus + Nothing = Everything*

OTHER CROSSWAY BOOKS BY PHIL RYKEN:

King Solomon: The Temptations of Money, Sex, and Power (2011)

Ecclesiastes: Why Everything Matters, Preaching the Word Commentary (2010)

The Prayer of Our Lord (2007)

Exodus: Saved for God's Glory, Preaching the Word Commentary (2005)

LOVING THE WAY JESUS LOVES

PHIL RYKEN

WHEATON, ILLINOIS

To Lisa Maxwell
my one, first, and only true love
and
To Jesus Christ
the eternal source of all true love

CONTENTS

PREFACE

"To write on the love of God is the Christian theologian's supreme privilege and supreme responsibility." Thus says Kevin Vanhoozer, who teaches theology at Wheaton College. In addition to a privilege and a responsibility, to write on the love of God is also this: a theologian's supreme humiliation.

Presumably, only a lover is able to write about love. Yet if there is one area of my life where I know that I fall short of the character of Christ, it is having true love for God and my neighbor. Nevertheless, my sometimes loveless heart is compelled to testify to the truth of God's love in Jesus Christ.

This book started with nearly the last sermon series that I preached at Philadelphia's Tenth Presbyterian Church. The heartfelt, Christlike love of that congregation helped sustain my ministry there for fifteen years. Yet for all the love that we shared as a church family, we still found that we had seemingly infinite room to grow in the love of God. Studying 1 Corinthians 13 in a Christ-centered way helped us—as I hope it will help you—to learn how to love the way Jesus loves.

As a demonstration of their love, several friends and colleagues helped to improve this book as it made its way to publication. Lynn Cohick, David Collins, Lois Denier, Tom Schwanda, and LaTonya Taylor all read the manuscript, making needed corrections and suggesting numerous ways to strengthen the exposition and application of the biblical text. Robert Polen checked facts and offered administrative assistance. Nancy Ryken Taylor prepared the study questions. Marilee Melvin entered the final revisions. Lydia Brownback and other friends at Crossway edited the book and shepherded it to the press. These labors of love will help you see the love of Jesus more clearly in the pages of this book.

As I was studying 1 Corinthians 13, I read a testimony from World Harvest Mission that expressed my own need for more of the love of Jesus. A missionary wrote:

> Upon returning home from a day of relief supply distribution, I joined my three-year-old daughter in the kitchen. She was drawing a picture of our family. I noticed what appeared to be me standing somewhat at a distance from the rest of the family wearing what was clearly a frown. "Is that Daddy?" I asked. "Yes," came the sheepish reply. "Why am I frowning?" She said, "Daddy, you never smile anymore."

The man proceeded to ask for help. "Pray for me," he wrote. "I want to apply this message of God's love to this cold, hard heart." The missionary's prayer is my prayer, too, and I hope you will make it your prayer as you read this book: "Lord Jesus, apply the gospel of your love to my cold, hard heart."

Phil Ryken
Wheaton College

A NOTE ABOUT THE PHOTOGRAPHS

In the spring of 2010, Gene Schmidt brought an exciting art installation to the streets of Philadelphia. Entitled "Lovetown PA" (http://www.lovetownpa.com), the project involved setting up wooden stencils in various settings around the city, including Love Park, the home of Robert Indiana's iconic "Love" sculpture. These stencils spelled out the complete text of 1 Corinthians 13 in the New International Version.

Before coming to Philadelphia, Gene had undertaken another ambitious project called "Manhattan Measure." Like some biblical prophet, Gene had measured the length and the breadth of Manhattan with nearly thirty thousand bright red yardsticks, laid out end to end and then collected again. Each individually numbered yardstick was used only once. When they were stacked together and displayed in a gallery, the yardsticks formed a large, three-dimensional, blood-red cross.

I was preaching at Philadelphia's Tenth Presbyterian Church when Gene brought his wooden stencils to the City of Brotherly Love. I had recently finished a series of sermons on 1 Corinthians 13—the messages that form the basis for this book. Naturally, I was interested to learn that an artist was bringing the full text of "The Love Chapter" to life on the streets of our city, just as I had been praying that it would come to life in the hearts of our congregation.

Somewhere along the way, as I began to prepare *Loving the Way Jesus Loves* for publication, it occurred to me that we might have an opportunity to collaborate. I knew that Gene's artwork had been documented by another talented New York artist, Alicia Hansen. So I began to dream that some of these beautiful images could appear on the cover of this book, and maybe on the pages inside.

Alicia's beautiful photographs of "Lovetown PA" provide permanent documentation of a temporary art installation. In showing Gene Schmitt quietly going about his work, they situate the artist in urban landscapes that display the splendor and misery of a great city. They also give fresh power to the words of the biblical text by placing them in juxtaposition with the world that we live in today.

I am deeply grateful to both Gene Schmidt and Alicia Hansen for sharing their work, allowing it to grace these pages. I am equally grateful to Crossway for sharing our vision to illustrate the written Word with visual images. My hope is that Alicia's photographs of Gene's artwork will capture the imagination of everyone who reads this book and open windows to a fresh experience of the love of God.

1

NOTHING WITHOUT LOVE

If I give away all I have, and if I deliver up my body to be burned, but have not love, I gain nothing.
1 CORINTHIANS 13:3

And Jesus, looking at him, loved him, and said to him, "You lack one thing: go, sell all that you have and give to the poor, and you will have treasure in heaven; and come, follow me."
MARK 10:21

There is nothing I need more in my life than more of the love of Jesus. I need more of his love for my wife—the woman God has called me to serve until death. I need more of his love for my children and the rest of my extended family. I need more of his love for the church, including the spiritual brothers and sisters it is sometimes hard for me to love. I need more of his love for my neighbors who still need to hear the gospel, and for all the lost and the lonely people who are close to the heart of God even when they are far from my thoughts.

Everywhere I go, and in every relationship I have in life, I need more of the love of Jesus. The place where I need it the most is in my relationship with God himself, the Lover of my soul. What about you? Are you loving the way Jesus loves? Or do you need more of his love in your life—more love for God and for other people?

THE LOVE CHAPTER

One of the first places people look for love in the Bible is 1 Corinthians 13. It is one of the most famous passages in Scripture, mainly because it is read so often at weddings. Some people call it "the Love Chapter," which is appropriate because it mentions love (*agape*) explicitly and implicitly more than a dozen times.

First Corinthians 13 is the Bible's most complete portrait of love. A literature professor would call it an *encomium*, which is "a formal or high-flown expression of praise."[1] The Love Chapter is a love song for love, in which the apostle Paul establishes the necessity of love (vv. 1–3), sketches the character of love (vv. 4–7), and celebrates the permanence of love (vv. 8–13) as the greatest of all God's gifts.

As familiar as it is, this chapter is not understood nearly as well as it ought to be. For one thing, people usually read it out of context. Admittedly, they do sometimes begin reading at the end of 1 Corinthians 12:31, where Paul says, "I will show you a still more excellent way." This is a good place to begin, because chapter 13 *is* "the more excellent way" that the apostle had in mind. But there is a wider context to consider—a context that many readers miss. As Gordon Fee writes in his commentary, "The love affair with this love chapter has also allowed it to be read regularly apart from its context, which does not make it less true but causes one to miss too much."[2]

One way to make sure we do not miss what God has for us in 1 Corinthians 13 is to remember who the Corinthians were and what God said to them in this letter. If there was one thing the Corinthians needed, it was more of the love of Jesus. The church was sharply divided over theology, practice, social class, and spiritual gifts. Some said they followed Paul. Others followed Peter or Apollos—"my apostle is better than your apostle!" Then there were those—and this was the ultimate form of spiritual one-upmanship—who claimed to follow Christ. There were similar conflicts about ministry, with various Corinthians claiming that their charismatic gifts were the be-all and end-all of Christianity—"my ministry is more important than your ministry!" This was the issue in chapter 12, where the apostle reminded them that although the church is made of many parts, we all belong to one body.

So when Paul wrote about love in chapter 13, he was not trying to give people something nice to read at weddings. After all, the love he writes about here is not *eros* (the romantic love of desire), but *agape* (the selfless love of brothers and sisters in Christ). Instead of preparing people for marriage, then, the apostle was trying desperately to show a church full of self-centered Christians that there is a better way to live—not just on your wedding day but every day for the rest of your life. The Love Chapter is not for lovers, primarily, but for all the loveless people in the church who think that their way of talking about God, or worshiping God, or serving God, or giving to God is better than everyone else's.

Here is another mistake that many people make: we tend to read 1 Corinthians 13 as an encouraging, feel-good Bible passage full of happy thoughts about love. Instead, I find the passage to be almost terrifying, because it sets a standard for love I know I could *never* meet.

None of us lives with this kind of love, and there is an easy way to prove it: start reading with verse 4 and insert your own name into the passage every time you see the word "love." For example: "*Phil* is patient and kind; *Phil* does not envy or boast; he is not arrogant or rude. He does not insist on his own way; he is not irritable or resentful; he does not rejoice at wrongdoing, but rejoices with the truth. *Phil* bears all things, believes all things, hopes all things, endures all things. *Phil* never fails." Do the same thing for yourself and you will know how I feel: not very loving at all.

THE NECESSITY OF LOVE

The problem is that love ought to be the distinguishing characteristic of our Christianity. Love is the virtue, said Jonathan Edwards, that is "more insisted on" than any other virtue in the New Testament.[3] Paul certainly insists on it in 1 Corinthians 13:1–3, where he makes a logical argument proving the necessity of love. Love is so essential that we are nothing without it.

According to the canons of ancient literature, an encomium usually begins with a comparison in which the author takes what he wants to praise and compares it to something else. That is very nearly what the apostle Paul does in 1 Corinthians 13: he takes love and makes a series of conditional comparisons to show how necessary love is. Each comparison has something to do with spiritual gifts or accomplishments—things that talented and virtuous Christians either have or do. The point, according to Charles Hodge, is that "love is superior to all extraordinary gifts."[4]

Paul starts with speaking in tongues, which is a gift that some Corinthians had and some Corinthians didn't. But even if they *did* have the gift, they were nothing without love: "If I speak in the tongues of men and of angels, but have not love, I am a noisy gong or a clanging cymbal" (v. 1).

To "speak in the tongues of men" is to communicate spiritual truth through the miraculous gift of utterance in a human language. To "speak in the tongues of angels" is an even greater gift, for it is to speak the very language of heaven. Paul does not minimize that gift of celestial eloquence, but he does say that it is nothing without love.

Some scholars believe that when Paul spoke about a "noisy gong" he was referring to the hollow bronze jars that were used as resonating chambers in ancient theaters—a Greek and Roman system for the amplification of sound.[5] The point then would be that without love, our words produce only "an empty sound coming out of a hollow, lifeless vessel."[6] Others believe that Paul was referring to the gongs that were used to worship pagan deities, like the goddess Cybele.[7] If so, then he is saying that without love we are merely pagans. The image in this verse always reminds me of *The Gong Show*, a television program from the 1970s on which contestants were judged on their ability to sing or dance. If the judges didn't like a particular act, they would stand up and strike a huge gong to end the performance. Gongs can produce a lot of noise, but they do not make very much music.

Cymbals *do* make music, when used the right way. But if someone keeps banging a cymbal, the noise is deafening. No matter how gifted we are, this is what we become if we do not use our gifts in a loving way. No one can hear the gospel from the life of a loveless Christian. People just hear "bong, bong, bong, clang, clang, clang!" To bring the metaphor up to date, "If I network for the gospel but have not love, I am only a noisy blog or a meaningless tweet."[8]

In verse 2 Paul starts listing other gifts, many of which were discussed back in chapter 12. He mentions prophecy: "if I have prophetic powers." Someone with this gift can foretell the future, or has supernatural insight to interpret what is happening in the world from God's point of view. Paul mentions the gift of understanding "all mysteries and all knowledge." The word "all" is emphatic. The person who possesses this spiritual gift has a comprehensive grasp of the great mysteries of God, including his plans for the future, like the mysteries that the prophet Daniel revealed for King Nebuchadnezzar in Babylon. By "knowledge," the apostle means spiritual knowledge of biblical truth—something the human mind can know only by the revelation of the Holy Spirit.

The Corinthians possessed gifts of knowledge and understanding, as Paul has said several times in this letter (e.g., 1:5; 8:1). But someone who has such gifts is nothing without love. A man may have mystical insight; a woman may know the deep mysteries of God. But these prophetic and intellectual gifts are nothing without love. So Paul says, "If I have prophetic powers, and understand all mysteries and all knowledge . . . but have not love, I am nothing" (13:2). No one cares how much we know unless they also know how much we care.

Or consider the gift of absolute faith. Paul says, "If I . . . have all faith, so as to remove mountains, but have not love, I am nothing" (v. 2). The apostle is referring here not to the saving faith by which every believer first trusts in Christ for salvation but to the extraordinary gift that some believers have to trust God for what seems to be impossible, especially in the work of his church and the growth of his kingdom. Gennadius of Constantinople claimed that "by faith, Paul does not mean the common and universal faith of believers, but the spiritual gift of faith."[9] Anthony Thiselton takes what the apostle calls "all faith" and describes it as "an especially robust, infectious, bold, trustful faith . . . that performs a special task within a community faced with seemingly insuperable problems."[10] Such faith has the power to move mountains, as Jesus told his disciples. In other words, by the grace of God, faith is able to accomplish the impossible. But even that kind of faith is nothing without love.

In verse 3 Paul moves from the gifts we have to the good works we perform. Here his argument comes to its climax: "If I give away all I have, and if I deliver up my body to be burned, but have not love, I gain nothing." Both of these examples are exceptional. Not many people sell all their earthly possessions and give 100 percent of the proceeds to the poor. Not many people suffer martyrdom through a killing act of self-sacrifice. These are two of the greatest things anyone could ever do for Christ. Surely people who do them deserve some sort of reward! Yet even the greatest good works can be done without love. Instead, they may be done to feed our spiritual pride or to get something from God. Yet not even the terrible pains of a flaming martyrdom are enough. Unless we are motivated by genuine love for God, it all counts for nothing. His love is the only thing that matters.

Understand that when Paul gives us this list of things that are nothing without love, he is really including all of our spiritual gifts and so-called accomplishments. No matter what God has given us and no matter what we have done for God, it means nothing without love. God may grant us the gift of helping or hospitality, of teaching or administration. It may be our privilege to hold a position of spiritual leadership, serving as an elder or a deacon in the church. God may allow us to serve as a missionary or evangelist or servant to the poor. And yet, shockingly, it is possible to use our gifts for ministry without having love in our hearts for anyone except ourselves. We are so selfish that it is even possible for us to do something that looks like it is for someone else when it is really for us—to enhance our own reputation or feed our satisfaction with ourselves.

Paul is not denying the value of spiritual gifts or downplaying the importance of ministry in the church. Praise God for prophets and martyrs! But he is saying that every spiritual gift must be used in a loving way. What matters most is not how gifted we are but how loving we are. As Jonathan Edwards said, "Whatever is done or suffered, yet if the heart is withheld from God, there is nothing really given to him."[11]

Understand that this message is for people in the church. It is not for unbelievers primarily, but for gifted Christians who are actively serving in ministry. Rather than congratulating ourselves for all the things we do for God, or looking down on people who don't serve God the way we do, or thinking that we have it right and everyone else has it wrong, God is calling us to do everything for love. Otherwise, it is all for nothing.

THE MAN WHO THOUGHT HE KNEW HOW TO LOVE

As I read the opening verses of 1 Corinthians 13, I have to wonder what hope there is for me. I have not conversed with angels, as far as I know, or moved any mountains, or suffered unto death. I have done much less—very little, actually—and even what I did was done with a lot less love than I should have done it.

Yet I know there is hope for loveless sinners in the gospel. One good place to see this hope is in a story that Mark told about Jesus. Whenever we talk about love, we always have to go back to Jesus. The love in the Love Chapter is really his love. So as we study each phrase in each verse of 1 Corinthians 13, we will turn again and again to the story of Jesus and his love. We will never learn how to love by working it up from our own hearts but only by having more of Jesus in our lives. The Scripture says, "We love because he first loved us" (1 John 4:19). Since this is true, the only way for us to become more loving is to have more of the love of Jesus, as we meet him in the gospel.

Mark 10 tells the story of a man Jesus met on the road to Jerusalem. People usually call him "the rich young man," or "the rich young ruler," but for reasons that will become clear in a moment, we could also call him "the man who thought he knew how to love."

Whatever we call him, the man was interested in eternal life and assumed there was something he could do to gain it. So he ran up to Jesus, knelt before him, and asked this question: "Good Teacher, what must I do to inherit eternal life?" (v. 17). With these words, the man was raising the most important of all spiritual issues: eternal life. We are all destined to die, so if there is such a thing as eternal life, it is worth every effort to gain it. The problem, though, is that the man was making a faulty assumption. He assumed that salvation comes by doing rather than by believing. So he asked Jesus what he had to *do* to get eternal life.

This assumption is faulty because none of us is good enough to be saved by the good things we do. We have all done too many of the wrong things and not enough of the right things. Furthermore, even the right things we have done were done to some degree in the wrong way or for the wrong reason. So Jesus said to the man, "No one is good except God alone" (v. 18). No one is good: not the young man who was talking to Jesus, not you, not me, not anyone. Only God is perfectly good.

To prove this, Jesus rehearsed the standard of God's righteousness. "You know the commandments," he said to the man: "Do not murder, Do not commit adultery, Do not steal, Do not bear false witness, Do not defraud, Honor your father and mother" (v. 19). If these commandments sound familiar, it is because they come from the Ten Commandments that God gave to Moses on the mountain—his eternal law.

I want to consider these commandments from a slightly different perspective, however. These are not just the laws of God; they also display the love that God demands. Each commandment requires us to love our neighbor. When God says, "Do not murder," he is telling us to love our neighbors by protecting their lives. When he says, "Do not commit adultery," he is telling us to love people by safeguarding their sexual purity. And so forth. Preserving property, honoring someone's reputation or position in life—these are all ways to show love. We could take all the commandments that Jesus mentions and summarize them like this: "*Love* your neighbor as yourself." In fact, this is exactly the way that Jesus *did* summarize them in the Gospel of Matthew, when he said that the first great commandment is to love God with all your heart and the second great commandment is to love your neighbor.

So this was the answer Jesus gave the rich young man when he asked what he had to do to inherit eternal life. "I'll tell you what you have to do," Jesus said. "If you want to be saved by doing, all you have to do is love your neighbor."

"Well, that's easy enough!" the man thought to himself. "I've never killed anyone, or slept with another man's wife, or committed grand theft chariot." What he said out loud was this: "Teacher, all these I have kept from my youth" (Mark 10:20). If all it takes to gain eternal life is to avoid breaking the big commandments, the young man thought that he had done all of that. Jesus wasn't telling him anything that he didn't know already. He had learned it all in Sabbath school!

But understand what the man was really saying. If these laws show the love that God demands, then he was claiming that he knew how to love, that he had enough love in his heart already.

Is this what you would claim? Would you stand before God and say, "I've been loving people all my life"? We would never come right out and say it, of course, at least not in so many words, yet that is the way many of us operate. Most of the time, most of us tend to believe that we do a pretty good job of loving other people. So we rarely repent of our loveless hearts. We fail to make learning to love like Jesus one of our highest priorities. We forget to pray that the Holy Spirit would make us better lovers.

This was all true of the rich young man. Jesus showed him that he was not the lover he thought he was, and he did so by giving him a simple, straightforward test. "You lack one thing," Jesus said, conceding for the moment that the man really did keep God's commandments: "Go, sell all that you have and give to the poor, and you will have treasure in heaven; and come, follow me" (v. 21).

This was the generosity test for love. The man claimed that he had never defrauded anyone. Now Jesus was calling his bluff: "You've never defrauded anyone? Really? Let's put that to the test. What about the poor? As fellow human beings, as people made in the very image of God, they have a claim on your charity. Now, do you love them enough to give away what you have so that they can have what they need?" In demanding charity for the poor, Jesus was testing the man's love for his neighbor. At the same time, he was also testing the man's love for God. Was he still claiming his right to be the lord of his own life? Or would he relinquish all of his own resources and trust Jesus only?

Sadly, the man failed this test. The Gospel of Mark tells us that he was "disheartened by the saying" and "went away sorrowful, for he had great possessions" (v. 22). "Disheartened" is not an exact translation (the Greek word *stugnasas* indicates shock or dismay), but it tells the spiritual truth. This man's heart was on display. Although he thought he knew how to love, it turned out that he loved money more than he loved Jesus and more than he loved other people.

THE LOVING SAVIOR

My purpose in telling this story is partly to convince us that we do not love much more than this man did. In fact, if Jesus gave us the same demand—to give everything we have to the poor—most of us would quickly come up with a long list of reasons why we shouldn't. Not everyone is called to sell all their possessions, we would say. This man may have been told to get rid of everything he had, but his calling is not our calling. We have to provide for our families and take care of our own basic needs, not to mention give our money to support other kinds of kingdom work—not just feeding the poor.

All of these objections are reasonable enough, but the real issue for most of us is that we always want to place limits on our love. We are ready to give, but only when we have something left over. We are willing to care as long as it isn't too inconvenient. We are able to love provided that people love us back.

Really, we ought to admit that we do not love the way Jesus loves. We may be nothing without love, but unfortunately we are nothing like the lovers God wants us to be. The apostle Paul was willing to admit this. Notice that in 1 Corinthians 13 he uses the first person singular. Rather than saying to the Corinthians, "If *you* speak in the tongues of men and angels, and have prophetic powers, and so forth," he says, "If *I* do these things without love, I am nothing." The apostle is not simply scolding here but including himself and bearing witness to what he had learned about his own sinful heart. Paul had all of these spiritual gifts: tongues, prophecy, knowledge, and faith. He had given away his possessions and offered his own body unto death. Yet he knew it was all nothing and that he himself was nothing without love.

Sadly, unlike Paul the rich young man in the Gospel of Mark was not ready to confess the lovelessness of his sinful heart. This brings us to what may be the most remarkable detail in this passage. In verse 20 the rich young man boasted that he had kept all of God's laws for loving his neighbor. The Bible says that when the man said this, Jesus looked at him and "loved him" (v. 21).

This detail is remarkable because one of the hardest people to love is a self-righteous sinner who thinks that he has his spiritual act together. This rich young man was a know-it-all. He had such a high opinion of himself that he refused to confess his sin. Most of us would not have liked this man at all. But Jesus *loved* him. In fact, it was just because Jesus loved this man that he gave him the generosity test for love. He wanted him to see that he was not the lover he thought he was, that he needed more of the love of Jesus in his life.

This remarkable detail gives us a glimpse of the love that Jesus has for us. We are not any more lovable than the man who thought he knew how to love. But Jesus still looks at us with a heart of love. He helps us see that we are not the lovers that we think we are, either. But he does not stop there. By his death on the cross he offers forgiveness to our loveless hearts. Then he sends us the Holy Spirit so that we can start to love the way that he loves.

We are nothing without love—this is the message of 1 Corinthians 13:1–3. But Jesus *does* nothing without love—this is the message of Mark 10, and indeed of everything else in the whole Bible. It was love that brought Jesus down from heaven to Bethlehem, love that caused him to perform miracles and preach the gospel, love that led him through the sufferings of Calvary and the cross, and love that exalted him to glory. Jesus Christ is the eternal incarnation of the love of God. Therefore, it is with love that he looks at us now—as much love as he had for the man he met in Mark 10.

Earlier we saw how ridiculous the Love Chapter sounds when we fill in the blanks with our own names. It reads very differently, though, when we put Jesus in the picture. If 1 Corinthians 13 is a portrait of love, then it is really a sketch of the Savior we meet in the Gospels: "*Jesus* is patient and kind; *Jesus* does not envy or boast; *Jesus* is not arrogant or rude. *Jesus* does not insist on his own way; he is not irritable or resentful; he does not rejoice at wrongdoing, but rejoices with the truth. *Jesus* bears all things, believes all things, hopes all things, endures all things. *Jesus* never fails."

Paul encourages us to read the Love Chapter in a Christ-centered way by the dramatic shift he makes between verses one to three, where he speaks in the first person, and verses four to eight, where love is personified. First the apostle tells us what he cannot do without love; then he tells us what only love can do.[12] And the reason love can do all these things is that it has become incarnate in Jesus Christ.

Jesus is everything that I am not. He alone has "love divine, all loves excelling." This realization does not crush me; it liberates me, because the love of Jesus is so big that he loves even me. And because he loves me, he has promised to save me, to forgive me and change me. We *are* nothing without love. But when we know Jesus, who *does* nothing without love, he will help us love the way that he loves.

In a subsequent letter to the Corinthians, Paul testified to the life-transforming love of Jesus, which turns our affections inside-out by compelling us to stop loving ourselves and start loving others: "For the love of Christ controls us, because we have concluded this: that one has died for all, therefore all have died; and he died for all, that those who live might no longer live for themselves but for him who for their sake died and was raised" (2 Cor. 5:14–15)—the Savior who died and rose again so that you could live with his love.

I invite you to welcome his love into your life. Confess that you are not the lover you ought to be and ask Jesus to change your heart. Say something like this: "Jesus, you are everything that I am not. You are pure love, and I am only the loveless sinner that you always knew I would be. But in your perfect love, I pray that you would forgive my hateful sins and teach my loveless heart to love the way that you love."

2

LOVE THAT IS BETTER THAN LIFE

Love is kind.
1 CORINTHIANS 13:4

*But when the goodness and loving kindness of God our
Savior appeared, he saved us, not because of works done by us
in righteousness, but according to his own mercy, by the
washing of regeneration and renewal of the Holy Spirit, whom
he poured out on us richly through Jesus Christ our Savior.*
TITUS 3:4–5

The earthly sufferings of Elizabeth Payson Prentiss were painful
and prolonged.[1] She struggled her entire life with insomnia and
severe headaches that left her exhausted. She also endured the sorrow of loss: two of her children died in short succession. Afterwards, the grieving mother's frail health was nearly destroyed. In
the deep distress of her soul, she cried out: "Our home is broken
up, our lives wrecked, our hopes shattered, our dreams dissolved. I
don't think I can stand living for another moment."[2]

Yet during those dark and desperate days, when her pains and
losses led her to think that she could not live even one more day,
Elizabeth Payson Prentiss never lost her hope in the love of God. In
fact, during those very days she began to write a hymn asking Jesus
for more of his love. "More love to thee, O Christ," she prayed.
"More love to thee." Then she asked God to use her earthly sorrows
to teach her how to love:

> Once earthly joy I craved, sought peace and rest;
> Now thee alone I seek; give what is best:

This all my prayer shall be, more love, O Christ to thee,
More love to thee, more love to thee!

Let sorrow do its work, send grief and pain;
Sweet are thy messengers, sweet their refrain,
When they can sing with me, more love O Christ to thee,
More love to thee, more love to thee!

What Elizabeth Prentiss found, when she despaired of life itself, was a love that is *better* than life. Later she wrote: "To love Christ more is the deepest need, the constant cry of my soul. . . . Out in the woods and on my bed and out driving, when I am happy and busy, and when I am sad and idle, the whisper keeps going up for more love, more love, more love!"[3]

LOVE'S PORTRAIT

Where can a suffering soul find more love to Christ and more love for other people? We are finding such love in 1 Corinthians 13, the Love Chapter of the Bible, which the apostle Paul wrote to help the gifted yet divided church in Corinth learn how to love.

Paul began by proving that love is absolutely indispensable. Nothing else matters, only love. No matter how gifted we are, or what we do for God, we are nothing without love. Loveless prophecy, loveless theology, loveless faith, loveless social action, even loveless martyrdom are all equally worthless. Nothing can compensate for the absence of love. John Chrysostom would go even further. When he preached this passage to his congregation in Constantinople sometime during the fourth century, Chrysostom said: "If I have no love I am not just useless but a positive nuisance."[4]

The problem is that we are less loving than we think we are and a lot less loving than we ought to be. If we want to avoid making a nuisance of ourselves, therefore, we need to learn how to love. First Corinthians 13 helps by sketching the character of love: "Love is patient and kind; love does not envy or boast; it is not arrogant or rude. It does not insist on its own way; it is not irritable or resentful; it does not rejoice at wrongdoing, but rejoices with the truth. Love bears all things, believes all things, hopes all things, endures all things. Love never ends" (vv. 4–8).

Chrysostom called these verses "an outline of love's matchless beauty, adorning its image with all aspects of virtue, as if with many colors."[5] What makes these verses so beautiful is that they are really a portrait of Jesus and his love. The literary technique Paul uses here is called *personification*. He takes the idea of love and describes what love does, as if it were a person. But of course love *is* a person, because Jesus Christ is the incarnation of the love of God. Therefore, everything these verses say about love is characteristic of Jesus. His love is patient and kind; it is not arrogant or irritable; it believes and endures all things; it never fails. So if we want to know what the Love Chapter looks like when it is lived out, all we need to do is look at the person and work of Jesus Christ.

We see the loving humility of Jesus in leaving the glory of heaven to take on the flesh of our humanity. We see his loving patience with all the people who pressed around him for healing. We see his loving submission in Gethsemane, when, on his way to the cross, Jesus did not insist on his own way. We see his loving perseverance in the way he suffered for sin. We see his loving mercy in the forgiveness he offered his enemies. We see his loving trust in asking the Father to raise him from the grave. From beginning to end, our whole salvation is a story of the never-failing love of Jesus, the love of God for us in Christ—what C. S. Lewis called the "Gift-Love" of God.[6]

One way for us to see the love of Jesus is to illustrate the Love Chapter from his life and ministry. This will be our approach to studying 1 Corinthians 13, to take what this chapter says about love and see how Jesus shows us each particular aspect of love. Along the way we will trace the course of his earthly life, his saving death, and his glorious resurrection.

In following the chronology of Jesus and his love, we will not always follow the exact order of 1 Corinthians 13. This method seems appropriate for our study because this chapter is a portrait rather than a biography. First Corinthians 13 gives us a composite picture of love. To see that picture as clearly as possible, we will connect every word to Christ and then make further connections to our own lives. The love that Jesus has shown to us proves to be the same love that he wants us to show to others. He does not love us merely to love us but also to love others through us as we learn to love the way that he loves.

ON KINDNESS

We begin with an aspect of love that may seem like a slender virtue. The Scripture says that love is "kind" (1 Cor. 13:4). Most people appreciate kindness—especially when someone is kind to them—but we may not take it very seriously. We talk about being "kind to animals" or showing "kindness to strangers." To be kind is to share some candy or help a little old lady across the street. But if that is all that kindness does, then saying "love is kind" would give love much less praise than it deserves. In fact, if love is "kind" only in the conventional sense of that word, then the Bible would be putting love at a level we can all reach—even without the grace of God—because everyone is capable of showing at least a little kindness.

If we think that kindness is something small, however, then we must not know the full biblical meaning of kindness or understand the extraordinary kindness of God. Because when we study what the Bible says on this subject, we soon discover that kindness is a high calling, and that the whole story of salvation can be understood as a gracious outworking of God's extraordinary kindness to us in Jesus Christ.

The word that Paul uses for kindness in 1 Corinthians 13:4 is unique. This is the only place where it appears in the Bible or other ancient literature (apart from later Christian sources that presumably borrowed the term from Paul). The apostle had a way with words, and the word he seems to have invented in this case (*chresteuetai*) is a verb. So rather than saying, "love is kind," perhaps we should translate the phrase like this: "love shows kindness."[7]

This is a good place to mention an important feature of 1 Corinthians 13: the words this chapter uses to describe love are not nouns but verbs (there are at least fifteen of them). This means that when Paul says that love is this and isn't that, he is not giving us an abstract or philosophical definition. Nor is he describing a feeling we have in our hearts. Rather, he is talking about something that we *do*—love as an action, not an affection. As Henry Drummond wrote in his famous little book *The Greatest Thing in the World*, love is "not a thing of enthusiastic emotion" but "a rich, strong, vigorous expression of . . . the Christ-like nature in its fullest development."[8]

This profound truth—that love is an active verb—helps us understand the biblical teaching on love in a highly practical way. Many Christians worry that they do not feel a particular way toward God. "I know I'm supposed to love God," we say, "but I don't always feel very loving. Something must be wrong with my emotions! I claim to follow God, but sometimes I am not even sure I love him." Then we wonder how we can get more of that loving feeling for God.

The Love Chapter teaches us that love is as love does. "Unlike other loves," writes the French theologian Ceslaus Spicq, "which can remain hidden in the heart, it is essential to charity to manifest itself, to demonstrate itself, to provide proofs, to put itself on display."[9] This is not to say that love is something we never feel or that we should ever stop asking the Holy Spirit to fill our hearts with warmer affection for God. But when it comes to love, what we do with our deeds is every bit as important, if not more so, than what we say with our words or feel in our hearts. The apostle John said, "Little children, let us not love in word or talk but in deed and in truth" (1 John 3:18). Paul looked at love the same way. He believed in loving by doing, not just by talking or feeling. Love is the way we live for God even when we do not happen to feel particularly loving.

When Paul took kindness and turned it into an active verb, he started with a word that comes up fairly frequently in the New Testament: the ordinary noun for kindness (*chrestos*). We see this word in Galatians 5, for example, where it is listed with the "fruit of the spirit" (v. 22). We also see it in Colossians 3, where Paul mentions it as one of the virtues that Christian people should wear as part of our everyday spiritual wardrobe (v. 12). Elsewhere, he says that kindness is characteristic of the ministry of the apostles (2 Cor. 6:6) and commands us to be kind to one another (Eph. 4:32).

When we take these passages together, we see that kindness is one of the ordinary virtues of the Christian life. To be kind is to be "warm, generous, thoughtful, helpful."[10] To show that such kindness is a verb, Gordon Fee defines it as "active goodness on behalf of others."[11] Other commentators describe a kind person as someone who is "disposed to be useful" and "freely to do good to others"—definitions that emphasize the readiness and eagerness of kindness to engage in the service of others.[12] Lewis Smedes calls kindness "love's readiness to enhance the life of another person."[13]

Some commentators connect kindness to patience, which is also mentioned in verse 4. They think Paul has in mind kindness to enemies, to people who have treated us badly. Thus, in his exposition of this passage, John Chrysostom asked how we should respond to the angry resentments and vengeful passions of people who do us wrong. "Not only by enduring nobly," he said (that is where the patience comes in), "but also by soothing and comforting," so that we can "cure the sore and heal the wound" of a broken relationship.[14] Someone who is "too kind" is sometimes described as "killing with kindness," but according to Scripture, it is also possible for us to *cure* with our kindness, bringing hope and healing to broken people.

THE LOVINGKINDNESS OF GOD

The best way for us to learn this kind of kindness is to see it in the character of our God, whose love is always ready to enhance the lives of others.

The title for this chapter—"Love That Is Better than Life"—comes from something King David once said about God. David began Psalm 63 by declaring that his soul was thirsty for God, like a dying man in an arid desert. Then, as he began praising and blessing God, he explained why God deserved his worship: "Because your steadfast love is better than life, my lips will praise you" (Ps. 63:3).

The King James Version uses slightly different terminology. It reads: "Thy *lovingkindness* is better than life." The words "steadfast love" and "lovingkindness" are attempts to take the rich Old Testament idea of covenant love and express it in the English language. David was praising God for his absolute faithfulness in keeping the love promises that he made to his people by saving them and being their everlasting God. It was because of his lovingkindness that God made Abraham a great nation, delivered Israel out of Egypt, established the kingdom of David, rescued the remnant of his people from Babylon, and performed many other mighty acts of saving deliverance. What the Old Testament calls "lovingkindness" is nothing less than total salvation. And as David understood, to know such kindness is better even than life itself.

The New Testament speaks in similar terms, putting the kindness of God in the context of saving his people. The apostle Paul told the Romans that God's kindness leads us to repentance (Rom. 2:4). He said further that it is because of God's kindness that the gospel is preached to all nations (Rom. 11:22). But perhaps the fullest expression of God's kindness comes in Paul's letter to Titus:

> But when the goodness and loving kindness of God our Savior appeared, he saved us, not because of works done by us in righteousness, but according to his own mercy, by the washing of regeneration and renewal of the Holy Spirit, whom he poured out on us richly

through Jesus Christ our Savior, so that being justified by his grace
we might become heirs according to the hope of eternal life. (3:4–7)

Kindness is not to be underestimated! We may be tempted to see it
as something small, but here the Bible takes everything that God has
done for our salvation and calls his saving cure a kindness. Consider,
then, the lovingkindness of God, as summarized in Titus 3.

To begin with, the kindness of God is a *saving* love. The
Scripture says that when God's lovingkindness appeared—this
refers to Jesus coming into the world—"he saved us" (Titus 3:5).
The most general and comprehensive way to describe what God
has done for us is simply to say that he has saved us. Jesus is the
Savior, the one who brings deliverance from sin and death. He saves
us from the punishment our sins deserve, which is nothing less than
eternal damnation. When we say that God is kind, therefore, we are
saying that he has rescued us from an eternity in hell.

The kindness of God is also a *merciful* love—a love shown to
people who do not even deserve to be loved. Titus 3:5 makes it clear
that when God saved us, it was "not because of works done by us
in righteousness, but according to his own mercy." We do not save
ourselves. We cannot qualify for heaven on the basis of the righteous
things that we have done. Leo Tolstoy was right when he said he
had not fulfilled even one thousandth of God's commandments—
not because he didn't try to, but because he wasn't able to.[15] This
is our problem as well—we do not and cannot do all the righteous
things we know we ought to do. If God saves us, therefore, it is only
because of his kind and loving mercy. It is not because we are lovable, but because he is love.

Further, the kindness of God is a *life-changing* love. Titus 3:5
says God saves us "by the washing of regeneration and renewal of
the Holy Spirit." Regeneration is the inward work of God the Holy
Spirit that gives a lifeless sinner new and everlasting life. Here that
life-changing work is called "the washing of regeneration." This
reminds us of Christian baptism, the sacrament that uses water to

signify cleansing. When the kindness of God comes into your life, it washes away all your sins. It also makes you an entirely new person. This happens immediately when the Spirit takes control, but then it continues for the rest of your life. There is "regeneration," which is a new spiritual birth, but there is also "renewal," which is the ongoing work of the Holy Spirit. God is making us and remaking us as completely new people. We are not what we once were—praise God! We will not remain what we are—praise him again, for this is the kindness of God.

Once I heard a father say that he felt as though his son's body had been taken over by aliens. All of a sudden the boy was more respectful, obedient, contrite, disciplined, compassionate, and teachable—everything a father hopes for in a son. Then the father realized that he was right: his son had indeed been taken over by an alien and supernatural power. Someone *was* living inside him! It was the Holy Spirit of God in all his life-changing power.

God's saving, life-changing lovingkindness is also a *generous* love. In his kindness, God has sent us the Holy Spirit, "whom he poured out on us richly through Jesus Christ our Savior" (v. 6). This verse testifies to the triune kindness of God. There is one God in three persons, each person full of lovingkindness. We have already seen the kindness of the Son to come and be our Savior and the kindness of the Spirit to regenerate and renew us. Here we see the kindness of the Father to send us the Spirit through the Son. What the Bible especially emphasizes is the generosity of this gift. The Holy Spirit is something that God has poured out richly. The Spirit is the best of all gifts because he is the gift of God himself. And when God pours out this gift, it is not merely a trickle but a fountain.

There is so much more that we could say about the lovingkindness of God. Titus 3:7 explains why God has poured out his Spirit on us and into us: "so that being justified by his grace we might become heirs according to the hope of eternal life." This verse testifies to the righteousness and the graciousness of God's love. In our justification God declares that we are righteous. He forgives our sins through the atoning death of Jesus Christ. He also adopts us as his own beloved sons and daughters. The great Presbyterian preacher Henry Boardman said, "Adoption is the highest proof of love which one being can bestow upon another, except dying for him; and Christ has done both for us."[16]

Then God does something more: he grants us the inheritance of eternal life, promising that we will live with him in his glorious kingdom forever and ever. The lovingkindness of God never comes to an end, because he keeps acting graciously on our behalf forever. His kindness is an *eternal* love.

Once we experience the kindness of God—his saving, merciful, generous, life-changing, eternal kindness to us in Jesus Christ—we can never again think that lovingkindness is something small and insignificant. The lovingkindness of God extends on into eternity. It really is better than life, because when God saves us in his love, we will live forever.

BE KIND

Have you experienced the kindness of God? Are you able to say, "God has been so kind to me! God the Father has adopted me as his beloved child. Jesus Christ has changed my life. By his death on the cross he has forgiven all my sins. He has given me his Holy Spirit and promised me eternal life. I am a personal recipient of the lovingkindness of God."

Anyone who is able to testify to God's kindness is called to show his kindness to others. This is the practical point in both Titus and Corinthians. When 1 Corinthians 13 tells us that "love is kind," it is not just defining love for us; it is also telling us how to live. The same thing is true in Titus 3. The reason Paul tells Titus about the loving-kindness of God is to help people in his church learn how to love.

The context is important. Titus was the pastor in Crete, and the Cretans were not very kind. Apparently, they needed to be reminded not to say bad things about people or to get into useless arguments (Titus 3:2). This is not surprising, given what verse 3 says about the way they used to live: passing their days "in malice and envy, hated by others and hating one another." We ourselves could make the same confession, because we have the same spiritual need. We are not lovers by nature, but haters.

This is why we need the gospel message of God's saving kindness. When the apostle wanted to help people learn how to love, he did not simply give them a long list of do's and don'ts; he also told them the story of Jesus and his love—the life-changing kindness of God in Christ. When that story becomes our own testimony, through faith in Jesus Christ, then we ourselves can live with the same kind of love. As Paul Miller writes in his book *Love Walked Among Us*, "Love begins not with loving, but with being loved . . . we can only give what we have received."[17] Only through faith in Christ, therefore, can we begin to love the way Jesus loves. *Knowing* the kindness of God enables us to start *showing* the kindness of God.

Every day we have opportunities to enhance the lives of others through kindness, which in some cases may prove to be a *saving* kindness. Not that we could ever be anyone's savior, of course, or cleanse anyone from sin. It would be folly to try. But one thing we can do is introduce people to the Savior by telling them about Jesus and his love. The greatest kindness that we can ever show to anyone is to share the gospel. So be kind to neighbors and strangers in the kindest way: by inviting them to church, talking with them about spiritual things, and testifying to them about Jesus Christ. The loving work of personal evangelism is the greatest kindness in the world.

The kindness we are called to show is also *merciful* kindness, which means we show it to people who do not even deserve it. In the words of Lewis Smedes, "Kindness is the power to move someone self-centered toward the weak, the ugly, the hurt and to invest in personal care with no expectation of reward."[18] It is all too easy to divide the world between people who deserve our help and people who don't. If God divided the world that way, none of us would ever get any help from him, because none of us would ever deserve it. But we are the recipients of undeserved kindness.

Now we, in turn, are called to show selfless kindness to the very people who have been unkind to us. The gift love of God, writes C. S. Lewis, enables us "to love what is not naturally lovable."[19] When the Bible tells us to be kind to our enemies, as it often does, it almost always tells us to do them some kind of good (e.g., Matt. 5:44; Rom. 12:21; 1 Thess. 5:15; 2 Tim. 2:24). We are called not merely to put up with people but also to treat them kindly. Do not wait for others to be nice to you before you are nice to them, but treat people as kindly as God has treated you through the cross of Jesus Christ. "If I can write an unkind letter," wrote Amy Carmichael, "speak an unkind word, think an unkind thought without grief and shame, then I know nothing of Calvary love."[20]

What else can we say about the kindness God is calling us to show other people? It ought to be a *generous* kindness. Give more to gospel charity, not less. Spend more time—not less—with the sick and the homeless, with needy children and people in prison. Of course, there are times when mercy itself teaches us to say no to a request for help, because it will only fuel a destructive addiction or a life-impoverishing dependency. But instead of thinking, "How can I get out of doing this?" or justifying our desire not to get involved, our first instinct should always be to see if there is a way for us to help.

Sometimes our kindness can even be *life changing*, especially when we show people spiritual kindness. Usually we think of kindness in terms of performing some practical task to help a person with a physical need. But as Jonathan Edwards pointed out in his teaching on 1 Corinthians 13, we should try to show kindness to people's souls. How can we do that? Edwards said we do so by leading them

> to the knowledge of the great things of religion; and by counseling and warning others, and stirring them up to their duty, and to a seasonable and thorough care for their souls' welfare; and so again, by

Christian reproof of those that may be out of the way of duty; and by setting them good examples, which is a thing the most needful of all, and commonly the most effectual of all for the promotion of the good of their souls.[21]

Put simply, we show lovingkindness by sharing the Scriptures, by giving wise spiritual counsel, by offering gentle words of rebuke when such words are truly needed, and most of all by setting a godly example. These are all acts of kindness that the Holy Spirit can use for the good of other people's souls.

Our kindness could never be *eternal*, of course, the way God's is. Yet there is still a way for us to echo the everlasting kindness of God in our own lives, and that is never to stop showing kindness. If we keep being kind, it will make a difference for Christ and his kingdom. People usually think of kindness as something small, but if every believer made a personal commitment to lovingkindness, it would change the world. The lost would be found. The dying would be delivered. The undeserving would receive grace. The loveless and the unlovable would be loved with an everlasting love.

Tertullian tells us that in the days of the early church, pagans sometimes called Christians "chrestiani" rather than "christiani."[22] The two words sound similar, of course, but there was another reason for the confusion. *Christiani* means "Christians," but *chrestiani* comes from the Greek word for "kindness." According to Tertullian, even when believers were not known as the Christ people, they were still known as the kindness people, and this kindness pointed others to Christ.

What about us? Are we known as people of kindness, or do people more commonly associate Christianity with attitudes that are stingy, judgmental, and hypocritical? Our calling is to live with such love that kindness becomes synonymous with Christianity. Sometimes we say that people will know we are Christians by our love, but here is another way to say the same thing: they will know we are Christians by our kindness.

3

LOVE IS NOT IRRITABLE

Love is not irritable.

And when it grew late, his disciples came to him and said,
"This is a desolate place, and the hour is now late.
Send them away to go into the surrounding countryside
and villages and buy themselves something to eat."
MARK 6:35–36

Is there anyone who irritates you? Of course there is! Whether it is someone at home, at school, at work, on the highway, behind the cash register, or on the other end of the cell phone, there is always someone who gets under our skin.

Robert Browning captures the feeling perfectly and deliciously in his *Soliloquy of the Spanish Cloister*. As its title suggests, the poem is a first-person account told from the perspective of a monk in a Spanish monastery. The monk is watching Brother Lawrence work in a cloistered garden and is muttering unkind words about everything he does. Every little movement that Lawrence makes is an irritation to his fellow monk, from the way he waters his roses to the way he trims the myrtle bushes.

The irritated monk also describes what it is like to sit next to Lawrence at mealtimes and watch him gulp his orange juice, or hear him talk about the weather, or listen to his annoying questions. "What's the Latin name for 'parsley'?" Lawrence asks innocently. Irritated by the very question, the monk thinks to himself: "What's the Greek name for 'swine's snout'?" After dinner, Lawrence carefully polishes his platter and washes his sacred goblet, which he has marked with his initial, "L." The monk despises every action in this daily ritual, right down to the precious way Lawrence puts his plate back on his own personal shelf.

Browning's poem is true to life. With vivid imagination, he shows how irritated one person can get with another. It is not just what people do that annoys us but also the way they do it. Usually the reasons for our irritation are small: how people eat, what they talk about, the way they walk across the garden. At the same time, Browning shows where our little irritations may lead. By the end of the poem the monk is trying to figure out a way to trip Lawrence into committing a damnable sin or to make some deal with the Devil that will destroy the brother's soul.

By setting this poem in a religious community, Browning shows us something further, namely, that we are as likely to be irritated with our brothers and sisters in Christ as we are with anyone. The poem ends with the chapel bells calling the monastic community to evening worship. Even as he begins to recite the creed, the monk is still harboring hateful thoughts about Lawrence in his hypocritical heart. "Gr-r-r," he says—"you swine!"

IRRITABILITY DEFINED

Most of us tend to think of irritability as a natural response to life's little frustrations. We also tend not to worry too much about our irritability, although some Christians may perhaps be wise enough to make it a matter for prayer. When was the last time you asked the Lord to help you respond graciously to that special person who always annoys you?

We should take our irritability much more seriously, because it is the very opposite of love. We know this because 1 Corinthians 13:5 says that love "is *not* irritable." Irritability is the antithesis of charity. It is not merely a way of complaining, therefore, but actually a way of hating.

This is the first time we have considered one of Paul's definitions for love that is drawn from its opposite. As a reminder, we are not taking everything from the Love Chapter in order. As we study this portrait of love, we are connecting everything to the life of Christ, considered chronologically. But first we need to define our terms. Sometimes Paul defines love according to what it is, and sometimes he defines it according to what it isn't. This is a good way to define any term, by showing what it *is* as distinct from everything that it is *not*. Such a definition results in fuller and greater clarity.

Here Paul tells us that love is "not irritable." The term the apostle uses for irritability (*paroxunetai*) has a range of meaning. One standard Greek lexicon translates the word as "easily provoked."[1] The New International Version renders it like this: "easily angered." Similarly, Charles Hodge defines it as "quick-tempered."[2] Anthony Thiselton offers a more detailed linguistic analysis and concludes that the word can refer either to simple irritation, or to outright anger, or to anything in between. In the end, he offers the word *exasperated* as perhaps the best translation.[3]

David Garland gives us something a little more colorful when he says that love is not "cantankerous."[4] We could add other synonyms. Love is not grumpy or grouchy. Love does not get ticked off. Love does not go off on a rampage or a tirade. Love does not launch into verbal abuse, or give people the silent treatment, or get into a bad temper, or do whatever else it is tempting to do when we are angry or irritated.

Presumably the Corinthians were guilty of some or all of these sins. Otherwise, why would Paul take the trouble to tell them that angry irritability is a loveless sin? Given all the arguments they were having in their church about theology, idolatry, sexual immorality, and spiritual gifts, we would expect that the Corinthians struggled to control their anger. Quarreling makes people irritable.

We have the same struggle. Like the Corinthians, we are living in a fallen world full of fallen people, including people who irritate us, annoy us, and make us angry. These are all areas where we all need to grow, but I want to focus on irritability. When Paul said that love is not exasperated, he may well have meant to include out-and-out anger. But irritability is anger's trigger finger—what Lewis Smedes calls "a spiritual readiness to get angry."[5] If we can learn to address the first rising of anger in the heart, we can learn how to love the way Jesus loves.

AT THE END OF A LONG DAY

To illustrate this particular kind of love, consider a famous incident from the earlier days of our Savior's earthly ministry. Jesus was teaching and performing miracles by the Sea of Galilee. This was before he went to Jerusalem, died on the cross, and rose again from the grave. The Gospels tell of a time when the disciples were irritated and Jesus wasn't, and seeing the difference will help us learn how to love with his peaceable love.

It so happened that the twelve disciples were returning from their first short-term missionary trip. Jesus had sent them out two by two, without bread or money, to preach repentance, heal the sick, and cast out demons (Mark 6:7–13). By the power of God, the disciples had seen people turn away from their sins. People whose souls were dominated by demonic power had been delivered. People whose bodies were broken by living in a fallen world had been made whole. So we can imagine the excitement in their voices when Jesus debriefed them and they shared what God had accomplished through their ministry. As Mark tells us, "The apostles returned to Jesus and told him all that they had done and taught" (v. 30).

This mission trip must have been exhausting, and by the time the disciples were finished sharing everything that was in their hearts, they were spent. Jesus cared for them with loving compassion, offering rest and refreshment. He said to his disciples, "Come away by yourselves to a desolate place and rest a while." Mark goes on to specify why these men needed to "get away from it all" for a little while: "Many were coming and going, and they had no leisure even to eat" (v. 31).

Anyone who has ever served people in need knows that ministry abhors a vacuum. There are always more people who need more help, and sometimes we just need to get away. So Jesus and his disciples "went away in the boat to a desolate place by themselves" (v. 32).

At this moment it is hard not to envy Philip and Bartholomew and the rest of the disciples for the sweet privilege of going away with Jesus to rest for a while. Unfortunately, things did not go quite the way they hoped. After all, Jesus was the most popular man in Israel. Thus, there was a constant demand for his teaching and healing ministry. People followed Jesus the way the paparazzi follow movie stars, except without the cameras. When people looked across the lake and saw his familiar sail on the blue sea, they hurried along the shoreline to reach the place where his boat would land: "Now many saw them going and recognized them, and they ran there on foot from all the towns and got there ahead of them" (v. 33).

The disciples could be forgiven, I think, if they were a little disappointed to see the crowds gather, yet again, along the lakeshore. When would they get a chance to rest? Yet Jesus went straight to shore, and when he saw the huge crowd, "he had compassion on them, because they were like sheep without a shepherd. And he began to teach them many things" (v. 34). This teaching session went on all day, as his teaching sessions often did. Jesus went on and on, and the longer he went, the wearier and hungrier the disciples became. Finally, "when it grew late," they came and said to Jesus, "This is a desolate place, and the hour is now late. Send them away to go into the surrounding countryside and villages and buy themselves something to eat" (vv. 35–36).

From a merely human perspective, this suggestion sounds perfectly reasonable and absolutely practical. Doubtless the people *were* getting hungry. The disciples certainly were! Remember that they did not even have time to eat. It was also getting late in the day. Soon it would be much too late for all these people—thousands of them—to find anything to eat anywhere in the neighborhood. Really, it was time for them to go back home!

Yet as reasonable as their words may sound, the disciples were getting irritated and exasperated. Their impatience had been building for hours, until finally it boiled over, as anger does. When they finally spoke to Jesus, interrupting his sermon (!), they addressed him in the imperative mood. "Send them away," they commanded Jesus. Their tone makes it easy to imagine what they had been thinking to themselves and perhaps saying to one another before finally they told Jesus what to do—things like "I'm starving!" or "Why don't these people just leave us alone?" or "Doesn't Jesus know when to quit?"

Jesus had a different idea how to respond, and the more we look at what he said and did on this day, the more we see his heart of love. First, Jesus put the demand back on the disciples. "You give them something to eat," he said (v. 37). If the disciples wanted to take charge, well then, why didn't *they* provide dinner? The disciples thought the idea was preposterous, of course. Their somewhat sarcastic response is another indicator of their irritation: "Shall we go and buy two hundred denarii worth of bread and give it to them to eat?" (v. 37).

In the end, of course, it was Jesus who provided dinner for everyone, taking five loaves and two fish, praying for his Father's blessing, and then multiplying the food until "they all ate and were satisfied" (v. 42)—all five thousand of them. So Jesus provided bread for his people. Rather than getting irritated with the needy crowd or his pushy disciples, Jesus gave them manna in the wilderness.

AN ANATOMY OF IRRITABILITY

What can we learn from this story? Before we look at the love of Jesus, let's begin with the disciples and examine their irritation more closely, because their negative example can teach us many things about our own irritation.

First, the disciples show us *who gets irritated*: everyone does, including people who are busy serving the Lord. Remember that when Paul told the Corinthians that love is "not irritable," he was writing to believers in Christ who were active in their local church. Christians are as likely to get irritated as anyone.

The disciples are a perfect example (or perhaps I should say, an *im*perfect example). They had been serving the Lord by performing miracles and preaching the kingdom. Now they were watching Jesus work, sitting in the front row for his teaching and miracle working. But almost before they could come back down from their spiritual high, they were irritated with the situation and exasperated with Jesus.

If an apostle can get irritated while he is spending time with Jesus, then we can get irritated too. No matter who we are, or what we do for God, anger can be a real spiritual problem for us. Whenever we start to get exasperated, we should see this problem for what it really is: a failure to love. We know this because the Love Chapter tells us that love is *not* irritable. So who gets irritated? I do, if I am honest about the sin of my loveless heart.

The disciples also teach us *when we are likely to get irritated*. They were tempted to this sin at the end of a full day after a long trip, when they were tired and hungry. This happens to all of us. Physical weakness puts us in the way of spiritual danger. So if we find ourselves getting more irritated than usual, we may need to take the small but very practical step of getting something to eat and drink, or taking a little rest. This is also something for parents to keep in mind when their children are getting angry: taking proper care of them will help them fight against sin.

Notice as well that the disciples were tempted to irritation right after they had been successful in serving the Lord. This too is true to the Christian life, as anyone in ministry can testify. Some of the strongest temptations come right after we have been busy doing kingdom work, and the Devil is desperate to regain lost ground.

If we want to resist the temptation to irritation, therefore, we need to anticipate when we are likely to be physically or spiritually weak and thus in special need of prayer and the help of the Holy Spirit. Missionaries should pray for grace after a season of fruitful ministry. Students should pray for grace the day after a long night of study. Fathers and mothers should pray for grace before they walk through the door after a long day of work. When we are weak, we can be strong only by the power of God.

Another lesson to learn from the disciples is *how irritability treats other people*. Basically, it doesn't want anything to do with them. When the disciples were irritated about how long they had to wait for dinner, they wanted Jesus to send everyone away. This was not the only time the disciples tried to keep people away from Jesus: they did the same thing when mothers were bringing their babies for Jesus to bless (see Luke 18:15–17). When we are irritable, we want to get away from other people—our family members, our neighbors, our classmates, our coworkers—even if it means keeping other people away from Jesus, too.

Notice as well that the disciples expected people to use their own resources to solve their own problems. Rather than asking Jesus to help or offering their own service as part of God's provision for other people's practical needs, the disciples pushed needy people away. They cared less about the genuine welfare of people in need and more about the effect that other people's problems were having on them. The idea of sending the crowds away may have been proposed as a way of getting them something to eat, but (surprise, surprise) it was also a way of getting the disciples what they wanted (namely, a little peace and quiet). Sometimes even our way of helping someone turns out to be a little bit selfish.

This is how irritability treats other people: by putting what we want ahead of what they need and, if possible, by trying to avoid their needs altogether. The real problem is us, not them. We need to be honest about this, because often we blame the people around us for the way we respond. "He really makes me mad!" we say, as if someone outside of us were directly and totally responsible for our sinful attitude. This is not to say that other people are never annoying. Sometimes they are. But the spiritual issue for me is not how irritating other people are; it is how irritable I am.

If we are easily provoked, if we tend to get angry in the wrong way about the wrong things, and if our anger is out of proportion to the situation, this is clear evidence of a loveless heart. Jonathan Edwards was right when he said, "Love is backward to anger, and will not yield to it on trivial occasions."[6] So if we *do* get angry about trivial things—about the way someone else drives, for example, or about something someone asks us to do, or about something someone forgot to clean up or put away, or about anything someone else did (or failed to do) that makes our lives a little less convenient—the problem is our own failure to love. Rather than putting the blame onto someone else—"If she does that one more time, I swear, I'm going to make her regret it for the rest of her life, and she'll have only herself to blame!"—we need to confess our own need for more of the love of Jesus.

One more thing to learn from the disciples is *how irritability responds to God.* Our exasperation is not just a failure to love other people but also a failure to love God. As we have seen, the disciples tried to tell Jesus his business and then spoke to him rather sarcastically. Rather than picking up on what he was trying to teach them—namely, that he always has the resources to provide for our needs—they made a smart-mouthed remark instead.

Irritability is like that: it has a negative view of God. Refusing to seek God's help, irritability chooses instead to get angry. If money is running short, or time is running out, or problems are running out of control, the person who gives way to irritation does not trust God to provide what is needed. Rather than turning toward God in that moment, we exaggerate our problems and get exasperated with God.

To help us see what such irritability does to our souls, Lewis Smedes takes a famous saying from Augustine and paraphrases it like this: "We are irritable, O Lord, until we make our peace with you."[7] Irritability is directly connected to our relationship with God, which is one of the main reasons it is such a serious spiritual problem. Anger does not just hurt other people; it also hinders our own relationship with God.

A DEMONSTRATION OF LOVE

What irritable people need—what *we* need—is more of the love of Jesus. Thankfully, we see such love in Mark's story of the feeding of the five thousand. What we see is not only an example to follow but also a Savior to receive into our lives, a Savior who has the power to change anger into love.

Everything Jesus did in this story is exactly the opposite of what his disciples did. This is because Jesus is everything that we are not. He is the living demonstration of *non*irritability, which is simply another way of saying that Jesus is love.

In all likelihood, Jesus was every bit as tired and hungry as his disciples. Jesus was often worn out by the exertions of his ministry. This time, he had been preaching and healing all day. It was hard work, as any preacher can testify. I once heard a homiletics professor claim that one hour of preaching takes as much physical energy as four hours of hard physical labor. Yet rather than wishing the crowds away and getting irritated when they refused to leave, Jesus kept blessing them. When we see him feeding the five thousand with both daily bread and the Word of God, we see what love can do when it is not irritable.

Notice the way Jesus loves. His love is drawn to people in need. Rather than pushing them away, as the disciples did, Jesus brought them close. He did this when he first saw the crowd gathering on the shore and decided to leave the privacy of his boat and go to them. Mark tells us that Jesus did this because of his love: "He had compassion on them, because they were like sheep without a shepherd" (Mark 6:34). Jesus regarded their need as more important than his refreshment. This is what love does: it lets the needs of others set our agenda, rather than letting our agenda limit how much we are willing to serve—especially when our service may give people an opportunity to hear the Word of God. Whatever limits we decide to place on our service should not be determined by our selfish desires but by the will of God, by our other legitimate callings, and by what is truly merciful for the people who are asking for our help.

A well-known example of the way love moves us toward people in need comes from the life of Mother Teresa. The first time she rescued a leper dying on the streets of Calcutta—picking him up, feeding him, and cleaning him—the man asked her why she was doing it. "Because I love you," she said.[8] This *is* what love does: it moves us toward other people, not away from them, even when their needs are overwhelming.

In loving compassion, and with tireless sacrifice, Jesus kept teaching the people all day. Even when it was time for dinner and the disciples told him to send everybody home, Jesus was still drawn to them with a heart of love. So he performed his miraculous multiplication, feeding the multitude with five loaves and two small fish. Jesus did this by looking up to his Father in heaven, which is something else that love does: it trusts God to provide what is needed. One of the main reasons why the disciples wanted to send people away—and why they spoke to Jesus so sarcastically—was because they were thinking only in terms of their own resources. Needless to say, they did not have enough bread on hand to feed five thousand people. Neither did Jesus, but he trusted the Father to give him the miraculous power to provide.

The lesson to learn from this true story is *not* that if you have the right number of loaves and fish, you will be able to work miracles.

Instead, see where love finds the strength to serve: by trusting in the power and grace of God. When people come to us with problems that are beyond us—asking questions we do not know how to answer, or requesting something we do not have, or expecting us to do something we do not have the strength to do—it is easy to get irritated with them for approaching us. But love takes what it has on hand, lifts its eyes up to heaven, and asks God to make our lives a blessing to people in ways that go far beyond what we are able to give. This is the way that Jesus loves: by trusting the Father. In dependence upon the Holy Spirit and in conversation with God the Father through prayer, Jesus opened his heart to be filled with the triune affection of God.

LOVING THE LOVELESS

This is also the way that Jesus calls *us* to love. Where do we learn to love with gentle, peaceable, nonirritable love? We learn it by trusting the Father's love and praying for the help of the Holy Spirit, as Jesus did. We learn it as well by seeing the love that Jesus has for us. One of the remarkable things about this story from the Gospel of Mark is the way Jesus treats his own disciples. When they get irritated with him, he does not get irritated with them but treats them with the same compassion that he had for everyone.

The five thousand were not the only people who ate bread and fish that day. When Mark says, "They all ate and were satisfied" (v. 42), this may well have included the disciples, but if not, they certainly had plenty of leftovers! After everyone had been fed, the disciples "took up twelve baskets full of broken pieces and of the fish" (v. 43). This was a memorable object lesson in the power and provision of God: one basket per disciple. So perhaps we should call this incident "The Feeding of the Five Thousand and Twelve," rather than "The Feeding of the Five Thousand." Those irritable, irritating disciples were well fed because they too were loved by the love of Jesus.

Jesus has the same love for all his disciples. Even after all the times that I have been irritated or exasperated with God for what he has or hasn't done in my life, he never gets irritated with me or too tired to deal with me, but he keeps loving me. All of my irritating sins are covered by the cross where Jesus died for my sins. Your sins are covered too, because of the love of Jesus.

Now we are called to love the way Jesus loves, with a nonirritated, un-angry love. Some people are bound to irritate us each and every day. When they do, how will we respond? We will respond with love, if we have asked Jesus to put his love into our lives—a prayer he loves to answer. As Henry Drummond wisely said, "Souls are made sweet not by taking the acid fluids out, but by putting something in—a great love, a new spirit, the Spirit of Christ. Christ, the Spirit of Christ, interpenetrating ours, sweetens, purifies, transforms all."[9]

The sweet love of Jesus will make us willing to be bothered with other people's problems, including the problems of people we don't even know, who are suffering in the forgotten barrios, broken-down orphanages, and war-torn countrysides of a fallen planet. It will enable and empower us to love even when we do not think we have anything left to give. And it will help us keep trusting God when we are tempted to be as angry with him as with anyone.

When we have the love of Jesus, every irritation becomes another opportunity to love the way he loves. In his book *The Four Loves*, C. S. Lewis notes that the daily "frictions and frustrations" that we meet in our everyday relationships prove that our own natural love is not enough, that we need something more. Usually we think that what needs changing is whatever irritates us about someone else. Lewis gives several examples. "If only I had been more fortunate in my children," people say. Yet Lewis points out that "every child is sometimes infuriating." And, "If only my husband were more considerate, less lazy," the wife says, to which her husband replies: "If only my wife had fewer moods and more sense."[10]

And so on. In every one of us there are attitudes and actions that are bound to irritate someone. But this does not mean that we have to respond in anger. If we do get angry, then what needs to change is our own hearts, which need to be filled again with the peaceable love of Jesus.

A simple but marvelous illustration of nonirritable love took place during a baseball game between the Philadelphia Phillies and the Washington Nationals during the 2009 pennant race. Phillies fan Steve Montforto was sitting with his three-year-old daughter Emily when a foul ball curled back into the upper deck. Montforto leaned over the railing to catch his first and only foul ball—every fan's dream. But when he handed the ball to little Emily, immediately she threw it back over the railing and down into the lower deck. Everyone gasped. Montforto himself was as surprised as anyone to see her throw the ball away. But rather than getting irritated with his little girl, he did what a loving father should do: he wrapped his daughter up in a tender embrace.

This is the way God loves us. He puts gifts into our hands that we could never catch for ourselves. Without realizing what we are doing, sometimes, we throw them away. Yet rather than getting irritated with us, he loves us again. Then he gives us the freedom to go love someone else with the same kind of love. He even gives us the grace to go back to people who throw our love away and love them all over again.

Who are the loveless people that God is calling you to love? Will you love them the way that Jesus loves?

4

LOVE'S HOLY JOY

Love does not rejoice at wrongdoing, but rejoices with the truth.
1 CORINTHIANS 13:6

*Then turning toward the woman he said to Simon, "Do you see
this woman? I entered your house; you gave me no water for my
feet, but she has wet my feet with her tears and wiped them with
her hair. You gave me no kiss, but from the time I came in she has
not ceased to kiss my feet. You did not anoint my head with oil,
but she has anointed my feet with ointment. Therefore I tell you,
her sins, which are many, are forgiven—for she loved much. But
he who is forgiven little, loves little."*
LUKE 7:44–47

The year 2009 marked the five hundredth anniversary of the birth
of John Calvin, the famous Reformer whose preaching brought
truth, mercy, and joy to the city of Geneva. That summer, hun-
dreds of Christians from around the world gathered in Calvin's old
cathedral, St. Pierre, high on the hill overlooking Lake Geneva.
They gathered to worship God and to hear again the great truths
that the Reformation recovered for Switzerland and the world—
truths like the sovereignty of God, the unique and supreme authority of Scripture, and salvation by grace alone through faith alone
in Christ alone.

On the eve of Calvin 500, a rather different celebration was
taking place down by the shore, where three hundred thousand
revelers were dancing through the streets for Geneva's annual Lake
Parade. The mood was not lighthearted and fun but raucous and
rebellious. Alcohol flowed freely. Intoxication led to nudity and

indecency, both gay and straight. On the morning after, there was trash everywhere and—lying in the trash—the prone forms of partiers too messed up to make their way home.

The contrast between the two celebrations was stark. One celebration was centered on God, and it left people better equipped to live for Christ through the sufferings of a fallen world. The other was centered on personal pleasure, and it left people empty and alone. I was an eyewitness, and as I jogged along the lakeshore the following day, with the early morning sun sparkling on the water, a young man with bloodshot eyes was yelling into his cell phone at the top of his voice. He had been out all night, and he was far from happy about it, possibly because his so-called friends had left him behind.

What will you choose to celebrate, and where will it leave you? When you see other people making the wrong choice and then reveling in it, are you happy for the chance to feel morally superior, or are you brokenhearted by sin and longing to share the gospel? When the Bible talks about these decisions, it says that what makes the difference is love, for love "does not rejoice at wrongdoing, but rejoices with the truth" (1 Cor. 13:6).

TWO KINDS OF REJOICING

The apostle Paul wrote these words to the first Christians in Corinth. Like modern-day Genevans, the Corinthians were known for their material prosperity and casual immorality. Even after they came to Christ, therefore, they were tempted to rejoice in the wrong things. So Paul taught them about the choice that love makes for holiness.

The words *wrongdoing* and *truth* are such broad terms that it is hard to be specific about why Paul included them in his portrait of love. Jonathan Edwards paraphrased the verse like this: "Charity is contrary to everything in the life and practice that is evil, and tends to everything that is good."[1] Similarly, Gordon Fee sees *wrongdoing* and *truth* as two sides of the same general reality.

Love is *for* everything that is godly and *against* everything that is ungodly. He writes:

> The person full of Christian love joins in rejoicing on the side of behavior that reflects the gospel—for every victory gained, every forgiveness offered, every act of kindness. Such a person refuses to take delight in evil, either in its more global forms—war, the suppression of the poor—or in those close to home—the fall of a brother or sister, a child's misdeed. . . . It is not gladdened when someone else falls.[2]

When the Bible talks about truth, it is not talking merely about what we know, but also about what we do. Usually we think that the opposite of truth is falsehood. Yet the Bible commonly opposes truth to unrighteousness. This is not a "category mistake," as a philosopher would call it, but simply a recognition that truth is something we live and not merely something we believe. Christians are called to "practice the truth" (1 John 1:6) and walk in the truth (3 John 3). "We cannot do anything against the truth," Paul later wrote, "but only for the truth" (2 Cor. 13:8).

"The truth," therefore, is everything that is right and good in faith and practice. According to Edwards, "it signifies all virtue and holiness, including both the knowledge and reception of all the great truths of the Scriptures, and conformity to these in the life and conduct."[3] Such truth is opposed to injustice, immorality, or any other form of wrongdoing.

As we consider the meaning of 1 Corinthians 13:6, we need to ask why someone would "rejoice at wrongdoing." The most obvious answer is that wrongdoers love the wrong that they do. The gossip loves to tell a secret tale; the thief likes to take what belongs to someone else; the abuser enjoys hurting people; the sexual sinner loves the lustful act that brings physical pleasure, and so on. It is the sin itself that the sinner celebrates.

The precise wording of verse 6 points to a different meaning, however. Paul says that love does not rejoice "at" (*epi*) wrongdoing. If he were talking about the sinner's celebration of the sinner's own sin, we might have expected him to say that love does not rejoice "in" (*en*) wrongdoing. Instead, by saying that love refuses to rejoice "at" wrongdoing, he puts the sin somewhere outside the person who is doing the rejoicing.[4] In this context, therefore, what love refuses to do is to celebrate someone else's sin.

Sometimes people celebrate the sins of others because it gives them license to commit the very same sins. This was part of the dynamic at Geneva's Lake Parade; when everyone else is acting lewd or getting wasted, it is easy to join right in. But this is not the choice that love makes, because true love cares about the holiness of God, and therefore it is careful to avoid being tempted by the enjoyments of sin.

Yet Paul may have had something more specific in mind. Remember that in writing to the Corinthians he was addressing churchgoing people. Christians certainly are tempted to enjoy many sins that are hateful to God. But we are also tempted—maybe more than most people—to feel a little sense of satisfaction when someone else does something wrong, especially someone with whom we disagree. When a pastor from a different denomination or a rival ministry falls into scandalous sin, for example, or when a politician from the opposite end of the political spectrum gets caught in a compromising position, it is hard not to feel at least a little morally superior. There is a smug feeling of sinful happiness that comes only when someone gets caught doing the kind of thing we always suspected them of doing.

Love would never feel this way, however, because love does not rejoice at wrongdoing. "It delights not" wrote Henry Drummond, "in exposing the weakness of others."[5] What love does instead is to "rejoice with the truth." Here the word for *rejoicing* is not the same word that is used earlier in the verse, in connection with wrongdoing, but something more intense (*sunchairein*). In effect, the person who rejoices with the truth—not "at" the truth, but "with" the truth—has greater joy. The feeling that comes with knowing and living with absolute sincerity elevates the spirit and brings elation of the soul. This is love's holy joy, the joy that comes only from pursuing what is right and true but never comes from being happy about wrongdoing.

Some commentators say that Paul uses the definite article here because he is talking most specifically about the gospel.[6] On this reading, what the loving person celebrates is not just truth but *the* truth—the gospel truth, that Jesus died for our sins on the cross and rose again with the promise of everlasting life. The problem with this interpretation is that it runs the risk of reading too much into the word *the*. What the Bible seems to have in view is not simply the truth of the gospel but the truth in all its forms, which the loving person always embraces. This includes the truth of God's character, that he is a loving, holy, gracious, and righteous God. There is the truth of God's Word, that every part of every verse in the Old and New Testaments is totally, absolutely, and inerrantly true. It also includes the truth of creation, which everywhere testifies to the power and beauty of God. Then there are all the great truths of the Christian faith: the sovereignty of God; the triune being of the Father, the Son, and the Holy Spirit; the glorious destiny of a new heavens and a new earth; and so on.

Yet there is one truth at the heart of the Christian faith that does more to produce holy joy than all other truths. It is a truth to live by and a truth to love by—a truth to celebrate. This truth is the grace of God for lost and needy sinners. God's grace may not be the only truth that Paul had in mind when he said that love "rejoices with the truth," but no truth gives more holy joy to a loving heart.

SIMON AND THE SINFUL WOMAN

One good place to see this truth in the life of Christ—and to see the difference between rejoicing at wrongdoing and rejoicing with the truth—is in the story of what happened one night at dinner. It is the story of Simon and the sinful woman, and the question to ask about the story is this: Where do I stand in relationship to Jesus? Am I more like the religious person in this story or more like the sinner? As we see the interplay of holiness, truth, and joy, the story opens our hearts to the grace of God and helps us see what love can do.

According to Luke, one of the Pharisees—a man by the name of Simon—invited Jesus to dinner. We do not know all the reasons why Simon extended this invitation, but it becomes apparent that he was trying to determine whether Jesus was a true prophet from God (which, of course, he was). We also know that Jesus accepted the invitation, "went into the Pharisee's house and reclined at the table" (Luke 7:36).

This was a familiar place for Jesus to be. The Gospels frequently show Jesus at the dinner table. What was unusual in this particular case, though, was the juxtaposition of two entirely different kinds of people. Jesus often ate with the rulers of a synagogue or other local religious leaders—men who were intrigued by the ministry of Jesus and wanted to talk theology, though not always with the best of motives. On many other occasions, Jesus ate with tax collectors and other notorious reprobates that respectable citizens tried to avoid. People desperate for love were always drawn to Jesus, the "friend of . . . sinners" (v. 34).

Ordinarily, the Pharisees and the tax collectors had nothing to do with one another. Yet at one dinner table the two worlds collided. Here the story accelerates with a memorable scene:

> And behold, a woman of the city, who was a sinner, when she learned that he was reclining at table in the Pharisee's house, brought an alabaster flask of ointment, and standing behind him at his feet, weeping, she began to wet his feet with her tears and wiped them with the hair of her head and kissed his feet and anointed them with the ointment. (vv. 37–38)

Luke tells us that Jesus was "reclining at table." In other words, he was dining in the formal style of biblical times, leaning on one side with his feet stretched away from the table. To us it may seem surprising for an uninvited guest to show up at dinner, but a meal like this would have taken place in an open-air courtyard, not in some secluded dining room. So the woman walked up, as people often did, much the way that a passerby might stop at a picnic or a block party today.

What the woman did next was one of the most extraordinary things that anyone has ever done for Jesus. In all likelihood, she had heard Jesus preach. Perhaps she was in the crowd that only shortly before had heard him speak about John the Baptist and the kingdom of God (see vv. 24–30). Somehow the woman had heard that Jesus was at the dinner table. Quickly she had run home to retrieve her most precious treasure: an alabaster flask of fragrant perfume. She had an idea. While Jesus was eating dinner, she would bathe his feet in sweet perfume, giving him the most expensive treasure that was hers to give.

As she stood there, the woman was so overwhelmed with love and joy that she began to weep. Imagine how freely her tears must have flowed for her to feel the need to wipe Jesus's feet. Yet this is what happened. Liquid emotion was rolling down the woman's cheeks and splashing on her Savior's feet. Swiftly she took her long hair and began to wipe away the tears. Then she started kissing and kissing his feet (Luke uses an intensive verb that indicates repeated action).

To understand the intimacy and humility of this encounter, we need to know that in those days the care of someone's feet was a menial task reserved for slaves. There is also some reason to believe that in those days a respectable woman never let down her hair in public. This was something she did only in the privacy of her bedroom, in the sacred company of her beloved husband.[7] What this woman offered to Jesus, therefore, was much more than her perfume. Everything she did—from standing at his feet to kissing his feet—was done with holy extravagance. It was as if she and Jesus were the only two people in the world. Her treasure, her tears, her hair, her lips—it was all for him. The woman was pouring out her heart with the fragrance of her love.

SIMON SAYS

Simon was scandalized by all of this. What Jesus accepted as holy in its loving intimacy, the Pharisee regarded as inappropriate and transgressive. Though he was too polite to say anything out loud, inside he was offended and embarrassed. Luke tells us what he was saying to himself in the self-righteous privacy of his judgmental heart: "If this man were a prophet, he would have known who and what sort of woman this is who is touching him, for she is a sinner" (v. 39). These harsh words should remind us to be careful what we say within our hearts, where even one short comment can condemn us a thousand ways.

In making this remark, the Pharisee was saying something about Jesus, namely, that he was no prophet of God. Simon was dead wrong in his evaluation, of course, but based on his assumptions, it was a logical thing to say. He assumed that if Jesus knew who this woman was, he would have nothing to do with her. When Simon saw Jesus allowing her to touch him and kiss him, therefore, he could only conclude that Jesus did not know what kind of woman she was, in which case he did not have any special access to God or any revealed knowledge of the truth.

Simon was also saying something about the woman. Luke has already told us that she was "a woman of the city," which may be a roundabout way of saying that she was a hooker. Certainly she was a sinner—everyone agrees about that. When Luke calls her a sinner (v. 37), he does not put the term in quotation marks but tells us the plain truth about her ungodliness. Simon called her a sinner, too (v. 39), and the woman knew it herself. This is exactly why she was drawn to Jesus: she knew that she needed to be forgiven. Jesus knew the same thing. In fact, he went farther by saying that her sins were "many" (v. 47).

So in a way Simon was right about the woman and her wrongdoing, even if he was wrong about Jesus. But the Pharisee was also saying something about himself, and here is where he made perhaps the most serious mistake of all. By identifying the woman as a sinner, he put her in a category separate from himself, making a subtle but unmistakable claim to his own godliness. Notice that the words he uses to describe the woman are highly pejorative. That "sort of woman," he calls her (v. 39), which is another way of saying "not a righteous person like me."

Understand what Simon was really doing: he was rejoicing at the woman's wrongdoing. He was not rejoicing in the sense that he wanted to participate in her sin, necessarily, but in the sense that he was glad to use her sin as a way of confirming his own sense of righteousness. He rejoiced *at* her wrongdoing and let it fuel his own spiritual pride. As long as there is someone else around who seems to be a bigger sinner than I am, I am glad to tell myself that I am good enough for God.

Now if someone had told Simon that he was rejoicing at wrongdoing, he would have protested loudly that no one was more offended by misconduct than he was. This may come out in the language he uses in verse 39, where he complains about the way that the woman was "touching" (*haptetai*) the feet of Jesus. Sometimes this term has sexual connotations (e.g., 1 Cor. 7:1). Perhaps from the Pharisee's perspective, then, she was not just touching the feet of Jesus; she was fondling them. Far from rejoicing in this kind of thing, he was quick to condemn it.

Yet for all his apparent outrage, Simon was committing a sin of his own—a sin much more deadly than prostitution: the sin of pride. He was claiming the merits of his own righteousness, denying his personal need for grace, and thus failing to show love for the lost or to celebrate the truth of God's grace for needy sinners. As far as Simon could see, some people were not even good enough to be forgiven. By taking offense at something that Jesus considered holy, the only person that he really condemned was himself.

THE LOVELESS PHARISEE

If there is any one truth that I wish I could communicate more clearly, it is the abundance of grace that God has for anyone who has fallen into sin. Jesus had the same desire. The goal of all his teaching—a goal that he fully and finally accomplished by dying on the cross and rising with forgiveness for the world—was to help people turn away from their sin and accept the free grace of God. He made the choice that love makes, never rejoicing at wrongdoing but always rejoicing with the truth.

We see that kind of love here—not only in the way Jesus forgave the sinful woman, and defended her, but also in the way he challenged this holier-than-thou Pharisee. Jesus was absolutely committed to the truth, including the truth about Simon and his loveless heart. He wanted Simon to see the grace God has for sinners and to experience the love his grace produces in the life of anyone whose sins are forgiven.

To help the Pharisee see this, Jesus told a little parable that had the power to turn the man's world upside down. The story went like this: "A certain moneylender had two debtors. One owed five hundred denarii, and the other fifty. When they could not pay, he cancelled the debt of both. Now which of them will love him more?" (vv. 41–42).

The answer was obvious, yet whenever someone asks a question this easy, we usually begin to suspect that it is a setup. We can tell from the hesitation in Simon's answer that he was worried about falling for a trick: "The one, I suppose, for whom he cancelled the larger debt" (v. 43). For all his wariness, Simon was right: both men were forgiven their debts, but the one who owed nearly two years' salary would love the moneylender the most.

Jesus was giving a lesson in spiritual economics, showing the direct transaction between forgiveness and love: those who have been forgiven the most also love the most. But Jesus did not stop there. He went on to apply his parable in a personal way, the way a good preacher always does. The story of the moneylender and the two debtors was really about Jesus and the two sinners at the dinner table, one of whom was Simon the Pharisee (whether or not he knew it).

Jesus began his personal application with an ironic question. "Do you see this woman?" Jesus asked. Of course he saw the woman! Simon's gaze had been fixed on her from the moment he saw her. Then Jesus drew a contrast between what the woman did and what the Pharisee failed to do: "I entered your house; you gave me no water for my feet, but she has wet my feet with her tears and wiped them with her hair. You gave me no kiss, but from the time I came in she has not ceased to kiss my feet. You did not anoint my head with oil, but she has anointed my feet with ointment" (vv. 44–46).

The contrast was absolute. A good host would have kissed his guests on both cheeks and anointed their heads with oil. Simon had fulfilled none of the duties of ordinary hospitality. By contrast, the sinful woman had done things that were more humble in their service and more extravagant in their affection. Rather than using a towel and basin, she had bathed Jesus's feet with her tears and wiped them with her hair. Instead of kissing Jesus on the cheek, she had kissed his feet—a radical gesture of submissive love. Rather than anointing Jesus with oil, she had given him sweet perfume.

What did all of this say about these two people? What did their actions reveal about the condition of their hearts? According to Jesus, the difference was love, and what made the difference was forgiveness. This is what he said to Simon, for everyone to hear: "Therefore I tell you, her sins, which are many, are forgiven—for she loved much. But he who is forgiven little, loves little" (v. 47).

When Jesus talked about someone who loves little and therefore must have been forgiven little, he was talking about Simon. The Pharisee's heart was totally exposed. For all his theology and morality, the man simply did not know how to love. We know this because he did not welcome Jesus the way a lover would. We also know it because he rejoiced at the woman's wrongdoing, which is something love never does. Simon had never truly experienced God's grace in his own life, and therefore he could not celebrate that grace in the life of another sinner. Here is how Paul Miller explains the man's reasoning: "His shock over this woman stems from the belief that (1) he would never do anything as bad as what she has done and therefore (2) he is better than her, so (3) he doesn't need anything Jesus might have to offer."[8]

If we are honest, we have to admit that our own hearts can be every bit as loveless. Have you done even one thing this week that showed Jesus the extravagant love of a forgiven sinner? Have you rejoiced over his presence in prayer, kissing him with praise? Have you offered him any costly treasure that it was a sacrifice to give or extended any service to him that only a slave would offer? These are all things that love will do when it rejoices with the truth.

Then consider the way that you have treated other people. Are you fed up with "the sinner" in your life? Are you sympathetic with his sinful weakness, or are you secretly glad that you do not have the problems he has or give in to the temptations he faces? Have you given up on what God can do in another sinner's life? And what is your attitude toward people who are poor and needy? Are you inclined to think that they are responsible for their own predicament and therefore undeserving of your mercy? These are all things that love would never do, because it refuses to rejoice at wrongdoing.

WHERE LOVE COMES FROM

As we consider how little love there is in our hearts, we should go on to ask some practical questions: Where can I find more love? What will it take for me to grow in my love for God and for other people? How can I learn to love the way Jesus loves?

Based on what Jesus said to Simon, we know that love begins with being totally honest about our sin. Simon did not love very much, because he had not been forgiven very much. But the reason he had not been forgiven much was that he did not think he had very many sins to be forgiven. The same is true for us: if we do not love, it is because we are not honest enough about our sin to take it to the cross. The result is a self-righteousness that shrivels our souls.

What Simon needed—what we all need—is the same experience that the sinful woman had at the end of this episode, where Jesus loved her enough to forgive her. Rejoicing with the truth of God's grace, he said, "Your sins are forgiven" (v. 48). Then he sent her out with the assurance of her faith, the promise of his peace, and the joyful calling to love other people the way that she had been loved. "Your faith has saved you," Jesus said; "go in peace" (v. 50).

I am drawn to this love, or at least I want to be. Are you drawn to this love? Understand that Jesus has as much love for us as he had for the sinful woman and also for Simon, whom he loved enough to uncover the secret of his loveless heart. Jesus does not rejoice at wrongdoing but rejoices in the truth of God's grace. So he offers the forgiveness that will touch your heart and fill your eyes with tears. All the bad things you ever did—including the secret things that no one else knows and the things so wrong you can hardly bring yourself to think about them—were nailed to the cross when Jesus died.

Once you know what it means to be forgiven—really forgiven— you never need to look down on anyone else ever again. Now you can face the truth about yourself because you know—really know— that you are not righteous at all. You do not need to pretend that you are better than someone else to make up for how bad you feel for not measuring up. Your acceptance by God gives you the grace to accept others.

Once you know that God loves you as you are, you are free to make the choice that love makes: not to rejoice at wrongdoing but to rejoice with the truth that God has grace for other sinners. You are also ready to do what love does: you are ready to forgive, ready to serve, and ready to pour out the treasure of your heart for Jesus.

5

LOVE WAITS

Love is patient.
1 CORINTHIANS 13:4

Now Jesus loved Martha and her sister and Lazarus.
So, when he heard that Lazarus was ill, he stayed two days
longer in the place where he was.
JOHN 11:5–6

The old man and his wife sat together in the front seat of the car out in the garage. They were sitting and talking, as they had done so often over the past sixty years. But the woman had Alzheimer's now, so her mind often drifted back to her teenage years, when her mother had died and every night she would turn on the lights and put food on the table for her father to eat when he came home from work, or from the local bar.

Tonight she insisted on going back home to take care of her father. "Now sweetheart," her husband was saying to her kindly, "do you know what I am going to say to you?"

"Yes," she replied, "you are going to tell me that Dad died fifty years ago. But I feel it in my heart that he will be waiting for me. I'm not getting out of the car until you take me home."

"But sweetheart," her husband insisted, "we *are* home. We have a nice apartment here with our son."

"No!" she answered firmly—"not here, home!"

So the conversation went, until eventually their son came home and found them sitting out in the garage. "How long have you been here, Dad?" he asked.

"Oh," his father said, "about two hours."[1]

Many people find it difficult to remain patient while explaining something for two minutes, let alone for two hours. But this man had learned something it can take a lifetime to learn, if we ever learn at all. He had learned the patience of love.

LONGSUFFERING

The apostle Paul began the portrait of love that he drew for the Corinthians by saying, "Love is patient" (1 Cor. 13:4). The biggest challenge for us here is not to understand what Paul meant but to do what he said. Thus I am reminded of one of Mark Twain's witticisms: "It ain't those parts of the Bible that I can't understand that bother me; it is the parts that I do understand!" What the apostle says about the patience of love seems easy enough to understand, however hard it may be to put into practice. Yet before we see this aspect of love exemplified in the life of Christ and empowered in our own lives by the Holy Spirit, it is important to make sure we understand what Paul meant when he said, "Love is patient."

According to the King James Version, "love suffereth long." This translation points to one legitimate translation of the biblical word for "patience" (*makrothumei*): love is "longsuffering." In other words, it "patiently bears with provocation, and is not quick to assert its rights or resent an injury."[2] This is the kind of love that Jesus calls us to show to our enemies, and we will say more about it when we get to verse 7, which tells us that love "bears all things" and "endures all things."

Longsuffering is not just for enemies, however; it is also something we need to show our friends. The kind of patience that Paul mainly has in mind, writes Leon Morris, is "patience with people."[3] It is the ability to put up with the frustrations we face any time we have a relationship with someone who is just as flawed and every bit as fallen as we are. A good synonym is *forbearance*. Anthony Thiselton would like to use the term *long-tempered* and wonders why we do not have such a word in English.[4] Presumably this is because so many of us are short-tempered that the idea of someone being long-tempered hardly even occurs to us!

In defining *patience* it is important to remember that all of the virtues in 1 Corinthians 13 are verbs, not merely nouns or adjectives. Thus the patience that Paul has in mind is active. Perhaps the best translation reads like this: "Love waits patiently." The Bible teaches the same truth in other places. We find it in places like Ecclesiastes, which says that "the patient in spirit is better than the proud in spirit" (7:8). We find it in the New Testament, too. In his first letter to the Thessalonians, the apostle Paul urged his brothers in ministry to "admonish the idle, encourage the fainthearted, help the weak, be patient with them all" (1 Thess. 5:14).

In telling us to exercise patience, the Bible is simply calling us to imitate the character of our God, who is patient both in the sense of being slow to anger and in the sense of waiting for just the right time to do something. In his letter to the Romans, Paul says that God's "forbearance and patience" are part of his "kindness," which is designed to lead us to repentance (Rom. 2:4). Not only is patience one of the essential attributes of God, therefore, but our very salvation depends upon it.

How patient God is with us! He does not hold our sins against us—praise God!—or condemn us for our impatience, or destroy us before we have a chance to repent. Instead, he patiently waits for us to ask for our sins to be forgiven. Paul had experienced this divine forbearance in his own life. Although formerly he had hated the gospel and rebelled against the kingdom of God, eventually the Holy Spirit revealed the risen Christ to him. So when Paul testified about God's work in his life, he described that work as a display of the "perfect patience" of Jesus Christ that leads sinners to eternal life (1 Tim. 1:16).

Have you experienced the patience of God's love? Do not presume upon his longsuffering, but let it compel you to commit your life to Jesus Christ. Then obey God's call to be patient the way he is patient.

Do I need to say how hard it is to do this? Probably not. Most of us know how impatient we are. What we need more than the conviction of our sin, therefore, is the help of the Holy Spirit.

But in case we do need to be reminded of how impatient we get, John Sanderson has some questions to ask about the frustrations of life. "Why is it," he asks, "that tires go flat when we are in a hurry to keep an appointment? Or, why does the vacuum cleaner stop working the day when company is coming?" Then he asks the most important question of all: "Why are we so unhappy and frustrated when these things occur?"[5]

It would be easy to add more questions to Sanderson's list: Why did I get the roommate who is so messy (or such a neat freak)? Why does my child wait until nine o'clock the night before a major project is due to ask if I can take her to the store and get some poster board? Why did the most difficult person to deal with at work get promoted to become my supervisor? More seriously, why do the people who need the most spiritual change seem least open to the sanctifying work of the Holy Spirit? And to ask the biggest question of all: Why doesn't God hurry up and make everything right with this world?

The Corinthians must have been struggling with similar questions. Why would Paul have started his list of love's virtues with patience if not because this was an area where they needed to grow? Presumably the Corinthians were as impatient as we are. They were quick to judge one another (see 1 Cor. 4:5), but slow to wait for the Spirit's work in this weary world. Like us, therefore, they needed to be reminded that love is patient.

A COSTLY DELAY

One good place to learn the patience of love is in the story of Lazarus and the empty tomb. In John 11 Jesus takes his own sweet time to let a man die before bringing him back to life. Through it all, he displays his loving patience in order to show us why we should be patient too.

The story begins with a man on his deathbed. Lazarus of Bethany, who was the brother of Mary and Martha, was deathly ill. So his sisters sent word to Jesus, saying, "Lord, he whom you love is ill" (v. 3). This was not simply a statement of fact, but an urgent plea for assistance. Mary and Martha wanted Jesus to drop whatever he was doing so that he could come and save their brother. They had every expectation that he would come as quickly as he could, because they knew that Lazarus was someone Jesus loved.

Yet rather than recognizing the urgency of the situation, Jesus gave a seemingly indifferent, almost dismissive response. "This illness does not lead to death," he said. "It is for the glory of God, so that the Son of God may be glorified through it" (v. 4). But if Jesus meant by this that Lazarus did not have a fatal disease, he was dead wrong—because Lazarus did, in fact, die.

How exasperating it was, therefore, that Jesus waited for two whole days before going back to Bethany, where eventually he arrived four days late. From a merely human perspective, verses 5 and 6 hardly seem to make sense: "Now Jesus loved Martha and her sister and Lazarus. So, when he heard that Lazarus was ill, he stayed two days longer in the place where he was." We might have expected verse 6 to tell us that when Jesus heard that Lazarus was sick, he went straight to Bethany. If Jesus loved these people, then surely he would hurry up and help them! Instead, he made an intentional delay, which resulted in suffering and death. Jesus was perfectly happy about it too. He said to his disciples, "Lazarus has died, and for your sake I am glad that I was not there" (vv. 14–15).

If I had been one of the disciples, I would have been frantic with worry, desperate for Jesus to hurry, and upset that he arrived seemingly too late to rescue Lazarus. The first section of John 11 is like a scene from a suspense film in which one of the characters is so slow to do what desperately needs to be done that the audience starts yelling at the movie screen, trying to get him to move faster.

John does not tell us whether the disciples were impatient, but Mary and Martha certainly were. Their reproach is unmistakable. When Jesus arrived at the house, the first words out of Martha's mouth were, "Lord, if you had been here, my brother would not have died" (v. 21). Martha's strong faith in Jesus and his power to heal was mingled with regret that he had missed his opportunity to save her brother. Meanwhile, Mary was staying inside the house, perhaps to give Jesus the silent treatment. But when she finally did speak, she said exactly what her sister had said. For days, Mary and Martha had watched their brother's agonizing decline and wondered when Jesus would hurry up and get to Bethany. When he failed to show up on time, they let him know exactly what they thought about a delay so costly that it claimed their brother's life.

Through it all, Jesus was totally unhurried. Patiently he waited two whole days before leaving for Bethany. Patiently he explained that even though Lazarus was dead, he still had a plan to glorify God and to help his disciples believe in his name. Patiently Jesus told Martha that her brother would rise again, affirming her faith in the final resurrection of the dead while at the same time announcing his own power over the grave. Patiently he comforted Mary, letting her tears touch his heart with sorrow.

By this time a crowd had gathered around the tomb. They too were critical of Jesus for his poor timing: "Could not he who opened the eyes of the blind man also have kept this man from dying?" (v. 37). Yes, Jesus could have kept the man from dying—if he had arrived sooner instead of dilly-dallying for a couple of days!

Nevertheless, none of the effects of this delay mattered even one moment longer when Jesus finally stood in front of the tomb and gave the first of his immortal commands: "Take away the stone." Worried that he was much too late, Martha told Jesus that he had missed his chance: "Lord, by this time there will be an odor, for he has been dead four days" (v. 39). Patiently her teacher answered, "Did I not tell you that if you believed you would see the glory of God?" (v. 40). To prove it, Jesus gave his second command: "Lazarus, come out" (v. 43). By his miraculous power, simply at the sound of his voice, Jesus brought the dead man out of the tomb. Then what had seemed like a costly delay proved to be the perfect setup for a life-giving miracle: Lazarus was set free!

What this proves is not merely the patience of Jesus but also his love. There are testimonies to his love all the way through John 11— his love for Lazarus, for Martha and Mary, and for his disciples. If we were tempted to doubt that love when Jesus let Lazarus die, we must believe it all over again at the end of the chapter when we see the dead man come back from the grave. Whatever reasons Jesus had for delay, it was not that he did not care. In fact, by the end of the story, his patience proves to be an expression of his affection. As James Boice says in his commentary on this passage, the delays of Christ turn out to be the delays of love.[6]

GOD IS IN CONTROL

John 11 does something more than show us the loving patience of Jesus Christ. It also helps us understand why *we* should be patient— patient with God, patient with our circumstances in life, and patient with other people.

Why does love wait? First, because *God is always in control.* From the perspective of Mary and Martha, everything seemed to be out of control. Their brother was dying, and any help that God was able to give came too late to make a difference.

Similarly, our own impatience typically comes out whenever something is out of our control. Children get impatient with their parents: "You never let me do what I want!" Parents get impatient with their children: "When will they ever learn?" At school we get impatient with the time it takes to learn everything we need to learn before we can go out and do what God has called us to do. On the job we get impatient with coworkers who make it harder for us to do our work. In the marketplace we get impatient with people who are lazy or incompetent. On the weekend we get impatient with our friends when their interests do not align with our plans. It happens any time that other people fail to honor our agenda or meet our demands for efficiency: rather than waiting for God to work, we try to "play God" for other people.

Underneath our impatience with other people lies our impatience with God. When we truly surrender our homes, our jobs, and our relationships to the lordship of Jesus Christ, we are able to wait patiently for his timing. But until then, we are always struggling for more control and are very impatient when we fail to get it.

John 11 can help us by showing us that God is always in control, even when it doesn't seem like it. Throughout this passage Jesus is in total control. He knows the end of the story from the beginning. So when he first hears that Lazarus is sick, he declares that his sickness is not unto death. Two days later, Jesus is still in control, even though Lazarus is dead. So he says, "Our friend Lazarus has fallen asleep, but I go to awaken him" (v. 11). Other people were saying, "What's the use? Lazarus is already dead!" But the Lord of life was busy working his plan, even if it would take a miracle. Not even death is able to challenge his sovereign rule. To believe this is not only to know God but also to love him. As Jonathan Edwards said, love for God disposes us "to see his hand in everything; to own him as the governor of the world, and the director of providence; and to acknowledge his disposal in everything that takes place."[7]

This is one of the main things to remember whenever we start to get impatient: God is still in control. True love has the patience to see this. According to John Sanderson, "Our resentment is against the timetable which the sovereign God has assigned to us, a schedule based on a plan of which we are usually ignorant. It is this ignorance which brings about our frustration, the seeming senselessness of delay, loss, or failure. But this is the reason why impatience is such a noxious weed—it leaves God out of our thinking."[8]

Do not leave God out of your thinking! Instead, always believe that God is still in control. Believe this because, as James Boice once said, "even though we cannot see how the situation will end or why it has come upon us, we can know that it flows from Christ's love and is controlled by it."[9] Once we know this, and learn to live by it, we are ready to love people with the patience that comes from trusting that God is in control.

GOD IS AT WORK

Here is another reason to be patient: love waits because *God is at work*. It is not simply that God is in control but also that he is doing something good in the lives of his people. God is working things out for our good and for his glory.

At the beginning of this story, when Jesus heard that Lazarus was sick, he said that this illness was "for the glory of God, so that the Son of God may be glorified through it" (v. 4). At the end of the story, when Martha insisted that her brother was really and truly dead and doubted whether Jesus could do anything about it, he said it again: "Did I not tell you that if you believed you would see the glory of God?" (v. 40). All of the events in John 11 are driven by the same goal that drives the universe, namely, the glory of God.

If people believed this, they would see it: God is always at work to display his glory. To begin with, he was at work in his disciples, who learned about the patience and the power of Jesus. This entire episode was an opportunity for them to grow in faith. The very reason why Jesus was glad that Lazarus died was that it gave the disciples an opportunity to believe in his power over the grave.

God was at work in Martha's life, too. There was a time when her impatience with her sister had gotten the best of her, and she had given Jesus an earful about everything that was wrong about Mary (see Luke 10:38–42). But now she was ready to learn from Jesus and to grow in faith. "Even now," she said to Jesus—even now that her brother was dead—"I know that whatever you ask from God, God will give you" (John 11:22).

Jesus was also teaching Martha about the resurrection. She had thought that the dead would be raised only sometime in the future, but Jesus wanted her to know that he himself, in his own person, presently held power over death. "I am the resurrection and the life," Jesus said: "Whoever believes in me, though he die, yet shall he live, and everyone who lives and believes in me shall never die" (vv. 25–26). In response, Martha made her great confession of faith. Did she believe in Jesus? Was the Holy Spirit working faith into her mind and heart? "Yes, Lord," she said. "I believe that you are the Christ, the Son of God, who is coming into the world" (v. 27).

God was also at work in Mary's life. When she saw Jesus weep at her brother's tomb, she learned her Savior's passion for all who suffer. Then there were all the things that the mourners learned. God was at work in their lives, too, showing them his glory through one of the greatest miracles that Jesus ever performed.

God is always at work. He is in control, yes, but he is also working to show us his glory, helping us know him as he is. This is something to remember whenever we get impatient. Even if we do not understand what God is doing, we can believe that he is still at work. Trusting in the sovereign goodness of God will help us turn our attention to others in love rather than focusing on our own frustrations.

Even when life seems out of control, God is still at work. It happens every day. A husband and wife have car trouble on a lonely beach and get stuck for a whole day—a day on which they make a new friend and have a chance to share the gospel. A mother and daughter go from store to store, frustrated that they can't find the right school supplies—but at the last store they end up in line next to a woman who is anxious about her son's first day at a new school and needs spiritual encouragement. Then too there are all the ways that God is at work in our own lives. So often we are in a hurry for God to do his work in someone else, when in fact he is busy wanting to do something in us.

Rather than getting impatient with our problems, therefore, and with problem people, we need to practice the presence of God. Pray like this: "Lord, I'm so impatient right now that I can hardly stand it. But deep down I know that you are in this situation, not outside of it, and that you are doing something good here. Help me to see what you are doing, or at least to believe that you know what you're doing, even if I can't see it." God is always busy doing more spiritual good than we know and bringing more glory to his name than we could ever imagine. If we are wise, we will wait patiently for him to do his work, not letting our impatience get the best of us but letting the love of Jesus work through us to the glory of God.

SUFFERING BUT STILL LOVED

God is in control. God is at work. All this is true, yet knowing these truths does not mean that we will not suffer. This is another lesson that John 11 teaches us about patience: *love waits through suffering.*

Remember that one good way to translate 1 Corinthians 13:4 is to say, "Love suffers long." In fact, one of the very reasons why we have to be so patient is that there are so many sufferings in life. God uses these very sufferings, in turn, to produce patience and hope (see Rom. 5:3–4).

We see some of life's most painful sufferings in John 11: sickness, death, and sorrow. Everyone in this story suffered. Lazarus suffered on his bed of affliction. His dear sisters suffered the agony of watching him die and then of struggling to understand why God let it happen. Their friends shared these sorrows as a grieving community. They all suffered these things in spite of the fact—indeed, because of the fact—that Jesus loved them. This is a spiritual lesson in itself: the fact that we go through suffering does not mean that we are not loved by God.

Yet of all the people who suffer in John 11, no one suffered more than Jesus. We see this in the way he relates to Mary: "When Jesus saw her weeping, and the Jews who had come with her also weeping, he was deeply moved in his spirit and greatly troubled" (v. 33). The Savior's heart was touched by the sorrows of his friends. The vocabulary here indicates extremely intense emotion. The sadness Jesus felt for this loss and his rage against the horrors of death came from the depths of his soul. Then his emotional response took its natural course, as we see in the Bible's shortest verse—also one of its most remarkable: "Jesus wept" (v. 35). The reason for the Savior's tears was not lost on his fellow mourners, who said, "See how he loved him!" (v. 36).

None of this would have been necessary, of course, had Jesus simply returned to Bethany as soon as he heard that Lazarus was sick, or healed him from a distance. But Jesus was waiting patiently for the glory of God, even through suffering. The delay was as costly for him as it was for nearly anyone. But love waits.

Seeing Jesus suffer helps give us more patience in our own sufferings. While we are waiting for our suffering to come to an end, we are still covered by the love of Jesus. Jesus understands. He knows what it is like to have a costly delay in life. So when God calls us to wait patiently through suffering, the Savior he sends to help us and comfort us is a Savior who understands. This is something else to remember whenever we get impatient: Jesus knows and cares about our earthly struggles. Therefore, we must learn to interpret our circumstances in the light of his love and not to judge his motives on the basis of our suffering.[10]

ALL'S WELL THAT ENDS WELL

A final reason to be patient is that *God will make sure that everything turns out right in the end.* So love keeps on waiting and waiting for the day when God will wipe away all our tears.

The raising of Lazarus is one of the Bible's clearest signs that

God has the power to make everything right. Jesus could have performed a miracle right away, the moment he heard that Lazarus was sick. But that would only have been a miracle of coming back to health, not a miracle of coming back to life. God had a plan to make a more complete display of his mighty power. So Jesus waited for his Father with totally trusting faith. When the time was right to reveal his glory, he thanked the Father for hearing his prayer and commanded Lazarus to come out from the grave (vv. 41–43).

This was not the final resurrection, of course, because Lazarus would die again. But it was an unmistakable sign of God's power over death—a testimony that on the last of all days, the children of God will rise in immortal splendor, never to die again. This is the gospel hope that Jesus confirmed by his own resurrection. First, Jesus died on the cross to pay the price for all our sins. Then, on the third day, he rose again with the power of eternal life for all who believe in him.

When the risen Lord Jesus comes again, the dead will be raised and everything will be made right. Every injustice will be rectified. Every good deed will be rewarded. Every kindness will return to the glory of God. Every sin that was confessed and carried to the cross will be forgiven. Everyone who dies in Christ will rise again. And it will all turn out better than we ever expected or imagined. The apostle James tells us to "be patient, therefore, brothers, until the coming of the Lord" (James 5:7).

When that day comes, it will be hard for us even to remember what it was like to suffer on earth, or how long we had to wait for Jesus to come again. This must have been the way it was for Mary and Martha. Alexander Maclaren imagines how long the delay must have seemed while they were waiting desperately for Jesus to come and help. "For two days, eight-and-forty hours, he delayed his answer," Maclaren writes, "and they thought it an eternity, while the heavy hours crept by, and they only said, 'It's very weary; he cometh not.'" Then there were the long days of grief that followed, when Mary and Martha laid their brother in the tomb and mourned his passing. But "how long did it look to them," Maclaren wonders, "when they got Lazarus back?"[11]

As soon as Lazarus came back from the dead, their sufferings were over, and Mary and Martha discovered that the words of the psalmist are true: "Weeping may tarry for the night, but joy comes with the morning" (Ps. 30:5). Once our sufferings come to an end, the pain is only a memory, and we are caught up in the joy that God brings to life.

This too is something to remember whenever we get impatient: God will make everything come out right in the end. Jesus is never early and never late but always right on time. He is not indifferent to the suffering of a fallen world, any more than he was indifferent to Lazarus and his sisters. In his love, he has a plan to bring all our sufferings to an end. His great day will come at exactly the right moment. When it comes, we will see his glory. Then we will know that he was in control all along, working everything for good, even through suffering, and that there was never any reason for us to be impatient at all.

6

LOVE'S FULL EXTENT

Love does not envy or boast; it is not arrogant or rude.
1 CORINTHIANS 13:4–5

*Jesus, knowing that the Father had given all things into his hands,
and that he had come from God and was going back to God,
rose from supper. He laid aside his outer garments, and taking
a towel, tied it around his waist. Then he poured water into a
basin and began to wash the disciples' feet and to wipe them with
the towel that was wrapped around him.*
JOHN 13:3–5

A worker is defined by tools of the trade. When one of my sons
took his oral exam for kindergarten placement, he was asked what
his father did for a living. "He works on computers," the boy said.
It was true: in preparing to preach I did most of my work on a lap-
top. These days almost everyone works on computers, but the tools
for some trades are more traditional. An architect works with a
pencil, a straight edge, and a drafting table. A plumber works with
a bucket and a set of wrenches. A virtuoso violinist works with a
Stradivarius. Every trade has its tools.

When Jesus was a young boy, working with his father the car-
penter, his everyday tools were the hammer and chisel of a stone
mason. By the end of his life, when the time came for him to die, the
only tool he needed was an old rugged cross. But shortly before his
passion, Jesus took up the tools of a humble servant. He wrapped a
towel around his waist, took a basin of water, and washed the dirty
feet of his disciples.

With this simple act of infinite condescension, the Lord of the universe demonstrated the self-denying character of his saving work and called every one of his disciples to a life of humble service.

GENEROSITY, HUMILITY, COURTESY

In his extraordinary act of foot-washing affection, Jesus illustrated the apostle Paul's definition of love in 1 Corinthians 13: "Love does not envy or boast; it is not arrogant or rude" (1 Cor. 13:4–5). Stated positively, these closely related terms call us to generosity, humility, and courtesy—a lifestyle of considering other people more important than ourselves.

Each term is carefully chosen. As we shall see, Paul used the same vocabulary earlier in this epistle, when he was criticizing the Corinthians for the way they were treating one another. They were envious, boastful, arrogant, and rude—everything that love is not.

Here is something these words have in common: they all relate to how we handle the good things that happen in life.[1] Everyone knows how difficult it is to deal with the hard things that happen—the difficulties, the discouragements, and the disappointments—but sometimes it is just as hard to handle success. *Envy* is a sinful response to the success of others, while *boasting, arrogance,* and *rude* behavior are sinful responses to any success we have of our own.

Start with the success of others. The New Testament word for envy (*zelos*) more literally means "to burn or to boil." Thus Anthony Thiselton translates as follows: love "does not burn with envy."[2] Envy is the pain we feel over someone else's prosperity. It is "resentment of someone else's good, plus the itch to despoil it."[3] Rather than rejoicing with those who rejoice, envy has what Jonathan Edwards described as "a spirit of dissatisfaction with, and opposition to, the prosperity and happiness of others as compared with our own."[4]

Envy is really a form of hostility. It is not merely the desire to have something that someone else has, which is the sin of coveting (see Ex. 20:17). Rather, it is the desire to see our rivals lose what they have. To quote again from Jonathan Edwards, "Instead of rejoicing in the prosperity of others, the envious man will be troubled with it. It will be a grievance to his spirit to see them rise so high, and come to such honors and advancement."[5]

A clear example comes from the story of Joseph and his brothers, who were so envious of their brother's status as the favored son that they threw him down into a deep, dark pit. Another example comes from the life of Haman the Agagite. Haman had almost everything that any man could ever want. In the kingdom of Persia he was second only to King Ahasuerus himself. Yet Haman was deeply resentful when Mordecai the Jew refused to give him the honor he thought he deserved. Not content with his own elevation, Haman wanted to bring Mordecai down. So, when the king decided to single Mordecai out for special honor, Haman grew so envious that he came up with an evil plan to get Mordecai killed.

A simpler example of envy's animosity comes from the pages of the *New Yorker* magazine, in a cartoon that depicts two dogs talking together over drinks. "It's not just that dogs have to win," one of them says; "it's that cats have to lose!"

The Corinthians were guilty of this kind of envy. Back in chapter 3 the apostle had accused them of envy and strife. In a community that was characterized by sharp social and theological differences, the Corinthians were tempted to have a spirit of competition toward church members who had spiritual gifts that differed from their own. Instead of seeing the good in other people, they criticized others' gifts and diminished their accomplishments.

This is something that love never does. True love "does not begrudge the status and honor of another, but delights in it for the sake of the other."[6] To love is to do "nothing from selfish ambition or conceit" but in humility to count others "more significant" than ourselves (Phil. 2:3). When someone else is promoted, praised, or elevated, the loving person is fully content with his or her own situation in life and thus can take joy and satisfaction in someone else's success. How do you really feel when someone of equal or lesser ability advances beyond you? This is a test that envy always fails and only love can ever pass.

There are also some sins we need to avoid when we meet with our own success in life. As hard as it can be to watch something good happen to one of our rivals, it can be equally hard to handle our own good fortune in a godly way. The Scripture says that love does not boast, or brag. In other words, the loving person does not demand attention for his or her accomplishments. Indeed, it is impossible to love and to boast at the same time, because in boasting we demand the center stage, whereas love shines the spotlight of its affection on one of the other actors in the drama of life.

The difference between loving and boasting came home clearly to me in the spring of my sophomore year, when my new debate partner and I were on a roll. After defeating some of the top varsity teams in the state, we were looking for more success at the state tournament. I can't remember what I said, exactly, but it must have been boastful, because one of my debate coaches said, "Phil, don't toot your own horn. Let me tell everyone how great you are." My coach was telling me not to boast, of course, but he was also giving me a good example of what love does, because his rebuke made it clear that he cared about me and wanted me to do well.

Boasting is a sin of speech, in which we use our words to make sure that people notice how great we are. Lewis Smedes calls it "our private advertising business, our little campaign to publicize an *image* of ourselves."[7] But "what comes out of the mouth proceeds from the heart" (Matt. 15:18), so Paul also makes sure to mention arrogance, which is a sin of attitude. The image behind the New Testament word for arrogance (*phusiosis*) is of something that is puffed up. So perhaps Anthony Thiselton's translation is the best: love does not "inflate its own importance."[8]

Here is something else that love does not do: behave rudely or obnoxiously. The word *rude* (*aschemonei*) can be used to refer to virtually any form of indecency or impropriety—anything from bad manners to shameful sexual sin. In this particular context, where Paul has been talking about envy and arrogance, he seems to be using the word to describe the bad way we treat people when we think that we are better than they are. To quote again from Lewis Smedes, "Arrogance drives us to be rude to people who have nothing to offer us, nothing to help us look good."[9] Using bad manners may seem like a small failing, if we think it is a failing at all. But the Bible says that when we do not treat people nicely and properly we are failing to love, which is always our calling, even in the little things.

It is apparent from many things Paul said in this letter that the Corinthians were guilty of these very sins. Some of them boasted of their superior wisdom and knowledge (1 Cor. 3:18; 14:2), or bragged that they were more spiritual than their brothers and sisters (14:37). Other church members had an overinflated sense of their own importance. Throughout his letter, Paul repeatedly uses the vocabulary of arrogance to show how puffed up they were with pride. "You are arrogant!" he said (5:2).

By using the same terminology in chapter 13, Paul was showing the Corinthians that the root of their spiritual problem was a lack of love. This is our problem, too. Why are we green with envy when someone else gets what we want? Why is it so important to us for other people to praise our accomplishments? Why are we rude to certain people in certain situations? It is because we love ourselves the most, and because sometimes we hardly love other people at all.

EVERLASTING LOVE

What we need is more of the love of Jesus—a deeper awareness of his love *for* us and a growing measure of his love *in* us as we learn to love other people. We see this love on every page of the gospel, but nowhere do we see it more clearly than in the amazing thing Jesus did for his disciples in John 13.

At the end of his life, only hours before his sufferings, death, and burial, Jesus met with his disciples for dinner. John tells us that "when Jesus knew that his hour had come to depart out of this world to the Father, having loved his own who were in the world, he loved them to the end" (John 13:1).

This verse bears witness to the eternal love of Jesus Christ. With reference to the past, John tells us that Jesus had shown his love to his disciples. He had loved his own by performing miracles, like the feeding of the five thousand and twelve. He had loved them by forgiving their sins, like the woman who anointed his feet with her tears. He had even loved them by raising the dead back to life, as he did for Lazarus. As long as he was in this world, Jesus loved his own disciples.

But now that the time had come for his departure—now that it was time for Jesus to die on the cross for our sins, to be raised from the grave with the power of eternal life, and to return to glory at the right hand of the Father—Jesus would show his disciples even more of his love. He would "love them to the end," or, as it says in the New International Version (1984), he would show them "the full extent of his love."

What does it mean for the Son of God to love his disciples to the end? It does not mean simply to the end of his life or to the end of our lives, although both are true. It means something more: Jesus will love us to the very end of all things.[10] The word John uses for "end" is also the Greek word for perfection (*telos*). The eternal love that Jesus has for us will never end. Its perfection is everlasting.

But how, specifically, does Jesus show us this love? John 13:1 marks a major turning point in the story of the gospel. Jesus had just made his triumphal entry into the city of Jerusalem, the place where he went to die. Chapter 12 thus ended with him announcing that he had come to "save the world" (v. 47). Then Jesus proceeded to do exactly that: save the world by giving his life as the atonement for sin. So at the beginning of chapter 13, when John says that Jesus "showed them the full extent of his love," he was referring broadly to our Savior's saving work on the cross, through the grave, and up to the skies.

When Jesus died and rose again for his disciples, he also did these things for us. We are all his own—every one of us who has been born again by the Holy Spirit, who believes in Jesus Christ as Savior and Lord, and who is destined to live with God forever. If we are his own, this means that Jesus loves us, and has loved us, and will love us to the very end. When Jesus did what he did for our salvation—the cross, the empty tomb, and the glorious throne—it was all for love. It was all "because of the great love with which he loved us" (Eph. 2:4). Indeed, there is no greater love than this, "that someone lay down his life for his friends" (John 15:13), and then rise up to give them eternal glory.

LOVE ON ITS KNEES

This is all part of the wider context for John 13:1, which serves as an introduction to everything else that follows. When John says that Jesus loved his own to the very end, he was talking about the love that he showed in the full work of his salvation. Yet there is also a more immediate context for John's statement. The full extent of the Savior's love is encapsulated in the very next thing that Jesus did. Therefore, John 13:1 does something more than summarize the second half of the Gospel; it also serves as the perfect lead-in to what Jesus did for his disciples at the dinner table.

People often say that actions speak louder than words. Maybe they do. Lorne Sanny served with the Navigators for more than fifty years, primarily as a leader in the area of personal discipleship. His teaching made a difference for Christ in the lives of thousands of people. But when I overheard members of his church talking about his ministry, they remembered something that had made a more profound impression on them than anything that Sanny ever said: they remembered him taking off his coat and tie and changing a flat tire for a single mother after church one Sunday morning. Sometimes even a simple act of humble service can help confirm the truth of what we say.

The ministry of Jesus was like that: he not only talked the talk, but he also walked the walk. We see this in John 13, when our Savior took a towel and basin to wash his disciples' feet. Jesus was performing a living parable that showed his generosity, humility, and courtesy. He was making a dramatic display of the nonarrogance and nonrudeness of his nonenvious love, which never begrudges us any good gift but always keeps giving us more and more.

When Jesus performed this humble act of service, he was not forgetting who he was. On the contrary, he did what he did "knowing that the Father had given all things into his hands, and that he had come from God and was going back to God" (v. 3). Jesus knew that he was the one and only divine Son of God, who had come from glory and would return to glory. But far from holding enviously to his position, or treating people rudely and arrogantly, Jesus offered humble service to his disciples. John tells us that he "rose from supper. He laid aside his outer garments, and taking a towel, tied it around his waist. Then he poured water into a basin and began to wash the disciples' feet and to wipe them with the towel that was wrapped around him" (vv. 4–5).

None of these actions would have been customary for the lord of a dinner party. A lord did not stand at his dinner table; he reclined in noble luxury. A lord did not strip down to his undergarments; he wore beautiful robes. A lord did not pour water or hold a towel. He certainly did not wash anyone's feet! In fact, if anyone deserved to have his feet washed, it was Jesus, whose feet were washed by the woman at Simon's house (Luke 7:37–38), and later by Mary of Bethany (John 12:1–3). So Jesus was taking everything that anyone would expect and turning it absolutely upside down. The Lord became the servant.

Peter watched all this happen. He saw Jesus work his way around the dinner table, washing everyone's feet. But when it came time for his own feet to be washed, Peter questioned what Jesus was doing: "Lord, do you wash my feet?" (John 13:6). To paraphrase: "Lord, you're not going to wash my feet, are you?" In response, Jesus gave Peter the hint that although he didn't understand what Jesus was doing now, eventually it would all make sense (v. 7). But Peter wouldn't stand for it. He said to Jesus, "You shall never wash my feet" (v. 8).

This was typical of Peter, who always spoke his mind. But this time Peter's words betrayed the pride of an arrogant heart. He was rude to Jesus, telling him what to do. In his arrogance he was too proud to let Jesus serve him. He was boasting that he was too clean to need any cleansing. In other words, Peter was everything that love is not. In the words of James Boice, he was "humble enough to feel the incongruity of having his feet washed by Jesus" but not "humble enough to refrain from telling his master what not to do."[11]

In response, Jesus explained to Peter that he was acting out a parable of salvation: "If I do not wash you, you have no share with me" (v. 8). At this point, Jesus was no longer speaking in literal terms; he was speaking about his disciple's need for cleansing from sin. What he said to Peter is true for everyone: we must be washed clean from our sin.

Deep down, Peter knew that he was a sinner. Indeed, this is why he started to follow Jesus in the first place. So with typical bravado, he said, "Lord, not my feet only but also my hands and my head!" (v. 9). As far as Peter was concerned, if it was worth doing, it was worth overdoing. A moment before he had told Jesus not to touch his feet; now he wanted to be washed from head to toe.

Lovingly, Jesus told Peter that he still didn't have it right: "The one who has bathed does not need to wash, except for his feet, but is completely clean. And you are clean" (v. 10). To understand this comparison, it helps to know the customs of Bible times. When a guest was invited to dinner, he would take a bath and change into nice clean clothes before putting on his sandals and setting out on foot for the dinner party. By the time he arrived, his body was still clean, but his feet were dirty from the dusty road. So the first thing a good host would do was to have his servants wash the feet of his guests.

Jesus used this custom to make a profound spiritual point. When he said that Peter was clean, he was saying that Peter was already justified before God (unlike Judas, who was not clean at all; vv. 2, 10–11). But this did not mean that Peter would never sin again. Like the rest of us, Peter *would* sin again, and when he did, he would need fresh cleansing—not from head to toe, because his righteousness was complete by faith, but in whatever area of life he was still stepping into sin. James Boice explained it like this: "Peter is a justified person and therefore needs only cleansing from the contaminating effects of sin, and not pardon from sin's penalty."[12] Like a dinner guest who had bathed his body but then walked along a dusty road, Peter was fundamentally clean yet still in need of cleansing.

As we overhear this conversation, we should see how much love Jesus had for Peter, and for us. When Peter misunderstood what his Lord was doing, Jesus patiently explained it to him. When Peter told him to stop, Jesus did not get irritated but kept serving. When Peter misunderstood again and told Jesus to wash his hands and his face as well as his feet, Jesus kindly assured him of his salvation. In short, Jesus did what the Bible says that love does: he was patient and kind; he was not irritable. And when he proceeded to wash Peter's feet, Jesus proved that he is not arrogant or boastful or rude but generous and humble. Here was love on its knees,[13] the very love that would stretch out its arms to offer its life for our sins. Soon Jesus would show the full extent of his love by dying on the cross, but his love was already on display when he put a towel around his waist, filled a basin with water, and started to do the work of a slave.

Jesus treats us the same loving way. He does not get impatient with our misguided questions or angry with our repeated mistakes. He comes to us in love, kindly correcting us, patiently explaining the way of salvation, graciously cleansing us, and humbly serving our every need.

TAKING THE LOWEST PLACE

Then Jesus calls us to live with the same loving and humble service. When Jesus washed the feet of his disciples, he was setting a deliberate example, showing us how to love. Afterwards, Jesus put his robes back on, took his place back at the table, and said: "Do you understand what I have done to you? You call me Teacher and Lord, and you are right, for so I am. If I then, your Lord and Teacher, have washed your feet, you also ought to wash one another's feet. For I have given you an example, that you also should do just as I have done to you" (vv. 12–15).

Jesus was making an argument from the greater to the lesser. He is the Lord, as Peter and the other disciples rightly called him. Jesus Christ is the supreme ruler of everything there is, the Lord God of heaven and earth. Nevertheless, in spite of his high and majestic greatness—or maybe because of it—he takes the lowest place. This is the greatest possible condescension: the Son of God and Lord of the universe kneeling to serve and then stooping to save.

If Jesus has done this for us, then we should do the same for others. The logical and practical conclusion to what Jesus did and said is that we are called to serve the way the Great One served, and to love the way that he loves. Here is how Jesus clinched his argument: "Truly, truly, I say to you, a servant is not greater than his master, nor is a messenger greater than the one who sent him. If you know these things, blessed are you if you do them" (John 13:16–17).

We are not greater than Jesus is. In fact, we are much less. We are not divine but human, not infinite but finite, not sinless but sinful. Therefore, it is even more fitting for us to take the lowest place. If we are the followers of a foot-washing Savior, then no act of service could ever be beneath our dignity.

It is not enough simply to know these things, however. Our calling is to *do* them by setting aside our arrogance, dedicating our lives to loving service, and then receiving the blessing that Jesus has promised to give. "At the source of all Christian service in the world," writes Donald English, "is the crucified and risen Lord who died to liberate us into such service."[14]

Understand that when Jesus told us to follow his example, he was not instituting foot-washing as a sacrament of the Christian church (although some Christians do wash feet as a reminder of their Savior's humility) but calling us to an entire lifestyle of humble service. He was not handing us a towel and basin, necessarily, but inviting us to take up the tools of service wherever we find them. To come under the lordship of Jesus Christ is to follow his example of servanthood.

We will never do this if we are full of envy, because in our envy we only think about what we can get, not about what we can give. Envy wants to bring other people to their knees. Nor will we serve if we are boastful and arrogant, because then we will expect other people to get down on their knees and serve us rather than the other way around. We will only get down on our knees to serve when we are humble enough to go to the cross, confess our sins, and then ask Jesus to help us love the way he loves.

What are the tools of our servant trade? We serve others with our words, not monopolizing the conversation and always calling attention to ourselves but using what we say to encourage and edify, turning attention to others and ultimately to the grace of God. We serve by doing less talking and more listening. Rather than saying rude and boastful things like "Look at me!" or "I don't see why they gave that award to her," we are called to say humbler things like

"I'm so happy you received a promotion," or "I admire your gifts and the way you use them."

We serve others with our hands, as Jesus did. Some of us are called to serve at home, with a dishrag and a laundry basket. Some of us serve in the kitchen, using pots and pans to make meals for the homeless. Some of us serve by pushing wheelchairs and playing musical instruments for people at the nursing home. Some of us serve by building a home for orphans, or wrapping our arms around a child with special needs, or pressing a stethoscope to the chest of a little boy or girl who otherwise would never receive medical care.

There are millions of ways to serve, if only we are willing. What is the place in life where your service shows the humility of your Savior? Look for every opportunity to serve. Take the lower place. Do not think that service is a job for someone else rather than a calling for you, because the moment you say this, you are claiming to be greater than your Lord. Remember the service of Jesus, with a towel around his waist and his love on its knees. Then take up the tools of the servant's trade.

7

LOVE HOPES

Love hopes all things.
1 CORINTHIANS 13:7

Father, I desire that they also, whom you have given me,
may be with me where I am, to see my glory that you have given
me because you loved me before the foundation of the world.
JOHN 17:24

In the year 1453 the great city of Constantinople was under siege. Over its thousand-year history the capital of the Byzantine Empire had withstood countless attacks, but everyone knew that this time was different: the city would fall.

The invader—the Ottoman sultan Mehmet II—had more than one hundred thousand trained soldiers in his Turkish army, while the Christian emperor Constantine XI had barely seven thousand men to safeguard his city. For all its natural and man-made defenses—both by land and by sea—there was no way to protect Constantinople against the German super-cannon of the Ottomans, which could hurl thousand-pound cannonballs more than a mile with deadly accuracy and concussive force, or from the mile-and-a-half causeway that Mehmet cut across the Galatian hills to bypass Constantine's blockade and roll his warships straight into the Golden Horn. Soon "the eternal city," as Constantinople was called, would fall under Islamic control.

Mehmet scheduled his final assault for the twenty-ninth of May. As the sultan made his military preparations, the citizens of Constantinople were filled with foreboding. But on the night before their city met its doom, they gathered for one of the most extraordinary worship services in the history of the world.

There were many Christians in Constantinople, from many places and many church traditions. There were bishops, priests, monks, nuns, and laypeople from Greece, Rome, Russia, and the Holy Land. Although all of them claimed Jesus Christ as Savior and Lord, they were so deeply divided in doctrine and practice that none of them ever worshiped together. Yet on the night of May 28, 1453, they all gathered in the Hagia Sophia, which for more than a millennium had been the spiritual home of the Byzantine church. The emperor began worship by asking forgiveness from the bishops of the various churches present. Then everyone celebrated the sacrament of the Lord's Supper, proclaiming the atoning death of the risen Christ and demonstrating their communion with one another as members of his spiritual body.[1]

The service ended at midnight. Within a matter of hours the silence of the city was shattered by the sound of the Ottoman assault, and by late morning Constantinople had become Istanbul, the city of the Muslim Turks. Istanbul remains Islamic to this day. But for one brief moment before the city fell, the world witnessed one answer to the hopeful prayer of Jesus Christ for the unity of the church—the prayer he offered to his Father the night before he met his own doom at the cross. May they "all be one," Jesus prayed, "just as you, Father, are in me, and I in you, that they also may be in us, so that the world may believe that you have sent me" (John 17:21).

THE HOPE OF LOVE

The prayer Jesus offered in John 17 proves the truth of something Paul said in 1 Corinthians 13: "Love hopes all things" (v. 7). Anyone who dares to hope for the unity of the church, as Jesus did, is able and willing to hope for anything!

Remember the approach we are taking in this book: in order to learn how to love the way Jesus loves, we are studying 1 Corinthians

13, looking at each phrase in its context and then seeing how that particular aspect of love is demonstrated in the person and work of Jesus Christ. This time we consider a prayer that Jesus offered shortly after he washed the feet of his disciples and shortly before he was betrayed—a prayer that teaches us the hope of love.

Near the end of his encomium to love, as his poem comes to its climax, Paul says, "Love bears all things, believes all things, hopes all things, endures all things" (v. 7). This verse is puzzling because at first it seems to be saying something untrue, or even ungodly. It makes sense to say that love "bears all things" and "endures all things" because true love is longsuffering. But how can the Bible say that love "believes all things" or "hopes all things"? Does this mean that love believes things that are false, or vainly hopes for things that will never happen?

Not at all! Paul is not saying that love believes anything irrational or hopes for anything unreal, as if love were "infinitely credulous and utterly indiscriminate in its believing and hoping."[2] Instead, he is saying that because of the power and grace of God, love hopes in all situations, including situations that seem completely hopeless. Here is how Gordon Fee explains it: "Paul does not mean that love always believes the best about everything and everyone, but that love never ceases to have faith; it never loses hope."[3] So we could translate 1 Corinthians 13:7 like this: Love "never tires of support, never loses faith, never exhausts hope, never gives up."[4]

Another way to translate the Greek word for "all things" (*panta*) is "always."[5] Love never loses hope but is always hopeful about the goodness of God and his power to work in someone's life. Some commentators put the emphasis here on hoping in God and in the mercy he gives us in Jesus Christ. But given the context, where Paul has been talking primarily about our love for one another, it seems likely that he is also thinking about the hopes we have for other people (based, of course, on what God can do in them and for them). This is the way John Chrysostom (who for many years served as the pastor of the Hagia Sophia) took the verse, when he preached that hope does "not despair of the beloved, but even though he be worthless, it continues to correct, to provide, to care for him."[6]

As far as love is concerned, there are no hopeless cases. This is one of the reasons why the apostle Paul kept holding out hope for the Corinthians. For all the sin he saw in their lives, and for all the problems they had in their church, he still loved them enough to say, "Our hope for you is unshaken" (2 Cor. 1:7; see also 10:15).

There is no situation in life that is so dark or desperate that hope is not there, if only we have the love of Jesus. Love does not give up on people when they are struggling. It does not give in to despair in the face of extreme difficulty. It does not declare that someone's heart can never change or that a broken community can never be healed. So when a discouraging voice (maybe our own) says, "There's no hope," love answers back and says, "Oh, yes, there is. I know there is. There is always hope in Jesus!"

Love hopes all things. Understand that whenever we give up hope, this is really a failure to love, because love hopes. Love hopes that someone lost in sin will believe the gospel. It hopes that a broken relationship will be reconciled. It hopes that by the grace of God, sin will be forgiven, and forgiven again. It hopes that even after a long struggle, there will still be spiritual progress. It hopes that someone who has fallen away can be restored to useful service in the kingdom of God. It even hopes that when a body gets sick and dies, it will be raised again at the last day.

Love hopes all these things and then holds out that hope to the people it loves. Love is willing to hope because it desires the very best in someone else's life. It is able to hope because it puts its ultimate confidence in the God of love and in his grace for people in need.

THE WORLD'S MOST HOPEFUL PRAYER

Once again, I want to illustrate this aspect of love from the life and ministry of Jesus Christ, whose spirit was sustained by the hopefulness of his love. We see this in what may be the most hopeful prayer that anyone has ever prayed.

It was the last night of our Savior's mortal life on earth. If it seems strange that we are getting close to the end already, remember the structure of the biblical Gospels, which give fully one-third of their attention to the death of Jesus and all the events that immediately led up to it.

On the night that he was betrayed—just a little while after participating in the Last Supper—Jesus prayed for God's blessing on his disciples. He made intercession before his Father, offering petition after petition on behalf of the people he loved. As we listen to our Savior pray in John 17, we hear what he was hoping—not in the sense of wishful thinking, but in the sense of fully trusting what his Father would do.

So what did Jesus hope? *He hoped that he would be glorified.* Before God the Son became a man, he lived in the glory of heaven, where he was worshiped by angels. In taking on the skin and bones of our humanity, Jesus laid aside that heavenly glory. Yet he hoped to take it up again. He had every hope that after he died, his mortal body would become radiant with immortal splendor. So Jesus prayed:

> Father, the hour has come; glorify your Son that the Son may glorify you, since you have given him authority over all flesh, to give eternal life to all whom you have given him. And this is eternal life, that they know you the only true God, and Jesus Christ whom you have sent. I glorified you on earth, having accomplished the work that you gave me to do. And now, Father, glorify me in your own presence with the glory that I had with you before the world existed. (John 17:1–5)

These verses bear witness to the mutual glory of the Trinity, that the Father and the Son live to glorify one another within the Godhead. They speak of the power and authority Jesus has to grant eternal life, which he gives only to those who know him in a personal and trusting way. But these verses also show us the hope of Jesus to receive eternal glory. This must be a man who hopes all things, because he even hoped that after he died, he would be glorified.

Then Jesus turned his thoughts to his disciples—specifically, the original disciples who witnessed his earthly ministry and were with him at the Last Supper. As Jesus prayed to the Father, he recounted what he had done for his disciples:

> I have manifested your name to the people whom you gave me out of the world. Yours they were, and you gave them to me, and they have kept your word. Now they know that everything that you have given me is from you. For I have given them the words that you gave me, and they have received them and have come to know in truth that I came from you; and they have believed that you sent me. I am praying for them. I am not praying for the world but for those whom you have given me, for they are yours. (vv. 6–9)

Jesus made it clear that he was not praying for everyone. He was not interceding on behalf of the world generally but for his own people specifically. He was praying for the people his Father gave him—the ones who had the Word of God and believed in Jesus as the Son of God, the people who belonged to God.

Once he had identified his disciples, Jesus began to pray for them, turning his loving hopes into petitions. *Jesus hoped that his people would persevere.* So he prayed that God would keep them safe to the very end:

> All mine are yours, and yours are mine, and I am glorified in them. And I am no longer in the world, but they are in the world, and I am coming to you. Holy Father, keep them in your name, which you have given me, that they may be one, even as we are one. While I was with them, I kept them in your name, which you have given me. I have guarded them, and not one of them has been lost except the son of destruction, that the Scripture might be fulfilled. But now I am coming to you, and these things I speak in the world, that they may have my joy fulfilled in themselves. I have given them your word, and the world has hated them because they are not of the world, just as I am not of the world. I do not ask that you take them out of the world, but that you keep them from the evil one. (vv. 10–15)

During his earthly ministry Jesus protected his disciples from spiritual danger. But now that he was leaving the world—a world that would hate his disciples every bit as much as it hated him—Jesus had the loving hope that his Father would keep them safe from the Evil One.

After praying for his people's protection, Jesus went on to pray for their sanctification. *Jesus hoped that his people would be holy.* So he prayed: "They are not of the world, just as I am not of the world. Sanctify them in the truth; your word is truth. As you sent me into the world, so I have sent them into the world. And for their sake I consecrate myself, that they also may be sanctified in truth" (vv. 16–19).

As concerned as he was with his people making it to the end, Jesus was equally concerned with what kind of people they became along the way. He hoped that they would grow in personal holiness. To that end, he prayed that his Father would use his Word to do his work in their minds and hearts. As he prayed, Jesus had the loving hope that the Bible would do what it was designed to do and make his people holy.

Verse 20 marks a precious turn in our Savior's prayer. Up to this point, Jesus had been praying most specifically for his original disciples. But in verses 20 to 23 he began to pray for all the disciples who would come afterwards. On the night before he died for our sins, as he went to his Father in prayer, the Savior of the world had us in mind. *Jesus hoped that we would be one.* So he prayed for our spiritual unity:

> I do not ask for these only, but also for those who will believe in me through their word, that they may all be one, just as you, Father, are in me, and I in you, that they also may be in us, so that the world may believe that you have sent me. The glory that you have given me I have given them, that they may be one even as we are one, I in them and you in me, that they may become perfectly one, so that the world may know that you sent me and loved them even as you loved me. (vv. 20–23)

These petitions are based on the unity of the Trinity. In the same way that the Father, the Son, and the Holy Spirit are one in purpose and love, Jesus prayed that we would be united to him and to one another. Today we often see the church divided by doctrine and practice, but Jesus prayed that we would be united in our love for one another and in our sacred calling to show the world that Jesus is the loving Son that God sent to save the world. When Christians worship together across denominational lines, cooperate for city-wide evangelism, or respond to a natural disaster with coordinated relief efforts, we become the answer to our Savior's prayer for Christian unity.

Jesus ended his prayer by interceding for our everlasting salvation. *He hoped that one day we would enter his glory.* Here is how Jesus prayed for our entrance to our eternal home and our everlasting acceptance in the love of God:

> Father, I desire that they also, whom you have given me, may be with me where I am, to see my glory that you have given me because you loved me before the foundation of the world. O righteous Father, even though the world does not know you, I know you, and these know that you have sent me. I made known to them your name, and I will continue to make it known, that the love with which you have loved me may be in them, and I in them. (vv. 24–26)

This is how Jesus prayed for us and for all his disciples. He prayed for our protection, our sanctification, our unification, and our glorification. The reason I call this "the world's most hopeful prayer" is that none of these things is remotely possible without the supernatural work of Almighty God. We are too weak to keep ourselves safe from Satan's temptations, too sinful to sanctify ourselves, too divided to unite ourselves, and too dead to raise ourselves up to everlasting life. Nevertheless, Jesus dared to hope that we would become one holy and loving church, kept safe until the end of time, when we would live in the love of God for all eternity.

WHERE THERE'S GOD, THERE'S HOPE

What was the basis for this hope? What enabled Jesus to pray for so many seeming impossibilities? If we know 1 Corinthians 13, then we know the answer. It is love that hopes all things. Therefore, Jesus must have had the hope that comes only from the love of God.

John 17 is full of hope because it is full of love. Consider how much Jesus must love us to pray for us as he did. Sometimes we doubt whether we will make it to the end. We fear that we will fall away or that Satan will snatch us out of the hand of God. But Jesus loves us too much to bring us only halfway to glory and then let us turn back. Thus he lovingly prays for our protection. We have similar doubts about our sanctification. Sometimes we find it hard to believe that we will ever be free from some particular sin. But Jesus loves us too much to leave us in bondage, so he prays that his Word will make us holy. Then there are all the doubts we have about heaven and the resurrection. Is it really true that God will raise our bodies from the dust and bring us into his eternal glory? The truth is that Jesus loves us too much to let us die and decay. So he prays that we will be with him forever. Jesus prays all of these hopeful prayers with a loving heart.

There is another hopeful affection that runs through these prayers, and that is the love of the Father. Earlier Jesus had assured his disciples, "As the Father has loved me, so have I loved you" (John 15:9). It was because he knew this love that Jesus prayed in hope. We see this clearly in John 17:24 where he says to the Father, "You loved me before the foundation of the world." Here we catch an intimate glimpse of the triune love of God. Since before the beginning of time, the Father has always been loving the Son. Jesus trusted that this love would continue, so that when he laid down his life for our sins, the Father would raise him back up again in glory. The hope Jesus had for his resurrection was not wishful thinking; it was based on the Father's love.

But that is not all. In loving the Son, the Father also loves all of the Son's disciples. As Jesus says to his Father in verse 23, you "loved them even as you loved me." Both the Father and the Son desire to draw us into the love of God.

To give an imperfect analogy, hearing Jesus pray to the Father is like a small child catching his parents kissing by the kitchen sink and thus getting a glimpse of the love that holds his family together. With wonder and delight, the child senses hidden depths to the love that his parents share and at the same time is drawn to that love and wants to join the embrace. Although the child cannot share every affection that his parents share, he nevertheless participates in their love.

So it is with the love eternally shared by the Father and the Son. We are included in the Father's love. This explains why Jesus dared to pray such a hopeful prayer. His prayer was grounded in the loving character of God. Jesus had the sure and certain confidence that his Father would hear and answer these prayers because he knew how much the Father loves us. It is love that hopes all things, and the hope we find in John 17 is founded on the love of the Father and the Son.

HOLDING OUT HOPE

Now the power of God's love puts the same hope into our hearts. As we love the way that Jesus loves, we are able to "hope all things" in the lives of the people we love.

We find this hope the same place that Jesus found it: in the Father's love, which we receive through the Holy Spirit. The reason that our "hope does not put us to shame" is that "God's love has been poured into our hearts through the Holy Spirit who has been given to us" (Rom. 5:5). This gift of love flows from the Father's heart. According to Jonathan Edwards, "Love tends to hope, for the spirit of love is the spirit of a child, and the more anyone feels in himself this spirit toward God, the more natural it will be to him to look to God, and go to God as his Father."[7] Are you hoping in the Father's love? Jesus said, "The Father himself loves you" (John 16:27). This promise is solid enough to serve as a foundation for life. Have you learned therefore to go to God for help the way a little child goes to a loving father?

Henry Drummond tells the story of a Scottish minister who went to the sickbed of a dying schoolboy. Upon leaving the room, the minister simply laid his hand on the forehead of the suffering boy, and said, "My boy, God loves you." The boy pulled himself up and, with all the strength that he could still muster, began crying out to everyone else in the house, "God loves me! God loves me!"[8] As a child of God, he was overwhelmed by the Father's love, and this filled him with newfound hope.

Our hope comes from the love of God the Father, and also from Jesus the Son. Jesus loved us enough to pray for us, asking that we could see his glory. More than that, Jesus loved us enough to die for us, giving his life for our sins, on the cross where he was crucified. Our hope springs eternal from the fountain of his undying love.

This hope will not disappoint us because it flows from the God of love. Hope is not simply wishful thinking. It does not depend on things working out the way we planned, or having our problems solved when we expect them to be solved. On the contrary, our true hope is Jesus himself, and the promises of his love. "At its core," writes Lewis Smedes,

> hope looks *beyond* a cure for disease, a solution for a problem, an escape from pain, for assurance from God that life has point and meaning in spite of disease, problems, and pain. Hope looks to the promise of the final victory of Jesus Christ over all that hurts and kills. This is the hope that gives a person courage to praise today and to face tomorrow with expectancy even when one does not expect the problem to be solved.[9]

This is also the hope that we hold out to others. Most of the time it is beyond our power to solve any major problems in the lives of the people we love. Believers keep struggling with sin. Families still have financial difficulty. Parents fight; children fail; friends suffer disease and death. But if we love people, we will not give up on what God can do.

When we have the love of Jesus in us, as Jesus prayed we would, then we will do for others what he did for us. We will not simply hope for the best, but because of the hope we have in Jesus, we will pray for the best. We will pray for others the same things that Jesus prayed for us in John 17. We will pray for preservation, that God will protect the people we love from the Evil One. We will also pray for their sanctification, asking God to use present trials to produce faith and hope and all the other graces of godliness. Then we will pray for their glorification, asking God to raise them up at the last day. I wonder: have you ever prayed specifically for someone to see the glory of God? This is part of what it means to "hope all things" for the people we love.

As we wait to see the glory of Jesus, we may even hope to see the answer to his hopeful prayers for the unity and the glory of the church. When I traveled to Turkey, I had the awesome experience of standing in the gallery of the Hagia Sophia and looking down at the sanctuary where thousands of believers once worshiped in the name of Christ—the very place where Christians from all over Constantinople gathered to pray as one people of God the night before the city fell into Muslim hands.

As I stood in that holy sanctuary, I was saddened to see that the Hagia Sophia is no longer used for Christian worship. Huge medallions in the name of Allah and Muhammad hang over the sanctuary. The altar at the front is turned at a perverse angle, facing Mecca—an unmistakable sign that honor and glory have been turned away from the one true God and given instead to a false prophet.

I was not just saddened by what I saw; I was angry. In this fallen world, there are many things to make us sad and angry. But as I reflected on what I saw, I began to have a hope that came from love. My hope was that one day my brothers and sisters in Turkey would be able to return the Hagia Sophia to its right and proper purpose—that they would be able to open its doors for people of all nations to fill its arches with praise to Jesus Christ.

What seemingly impossible things are you hoping for, not just in your own life, but also in the lives of the people you love? What hopes do you have for the ministry of your church, or for city neighborhoods in the grip of poverty, or for the advance of the gospel in distant lands? If your hope is in the God of love, then you are not just "hoping against hope," but hoping the way Jesus hopes because you love the way Jesus loves, as you wait to see what God will do.

8

LOVE IS NOT SELF-SEEKING

Love does not insist on its own way.
1 CORINTHIANS 13:5

Going a little farther he fell on his face and prayed, saying, "My Father, if it be possible, let this cup pass from me; nevertheless, not as I will, but as you will."
MATTHEW 26:39

It was a moment of brutal and unexpected honesty. A friend who shall remain nameless—okay, it was my brother-in-law Jeff—was in a worship service, singing as loudly as he could. Yet when people started to look at him strangely, he could sense that something was wrong. It was not his singing voice, which is pleasing and tuneful, but his lyrics. Everyone else was singing Adelaide Pollard's classic hymn: "Have thine own way, Lord! Have thine own way!" But without realizing it, Jeff was using a different and probably more honest pronoun. "Have *mine* own way, Lord!" he had been singing with all his might. "Have mine own way!"

With apologies to Walt Whitman, this is the true "Song of Myself"—the one that selfish sinners love to sing, even if we usually try not to sing it in church. Honestly, there are times in life when we would rather have things our way than God's way. Given the choice, we would prefer to take complete control of our looks, our health, our grades, our paycheck, and whatever situation in life is giving us the most difficulty. If our hearts could rewrite the song, it would go like this:

Have mine own way, Lord! Have mine own way!
Let me be in charge here, at least for today.
I really don't need you—say what you will;
I've got my own plan, Lord; you can just chill!

THE SELFLESSNESS OF LOVE

The selfish, self-centered way that most of us usually live is directly contrary to love, which the Bible says "does not insist on its way" (1 Cor. 13:5). "The spirit of charity," wrote Jonathan Edwards, "is the opposite of a selfish spirit."[1] Here is how the great theologian characterized the contrast: "Selfishness is a principle that contracts the heart, and confines it to self, while love enlarges it, and extends it to others."[2]

Unfortunately, many of our attitudes and actions are exactly the opposite of what they ought to be, and as a result, our hearts are constricted. This is one of the reasons why 1 Corinthians 13 is such a challenge for us. All of the things it tells us that love does are almost impossible for us to do, whereas all of the things it tells us that love never does are things we do all the time. This is because we love ourselves more than we love other people or even God. As he considers everything Paul says about love in 1 Corinthians 13, David Garland wisely observes that "each thing that love does is something in which the ego does not dominate," but "each thing that love does not do is something in which the ego does dominate."[3] Therefore, if we find it hard to do what the Love Chapter tells us to do and to love other people, this is a clear sign that our lives are dominated by selfish affections.

There is a limited sense, of course, in which we are supposed to love ourselves. When Jesus told us to love our neighbors as ourselves (see Matt. 19:19), he assumed that we would have the good sense to take care of ourselves. But he also refused to let us limit our love to the horizon of our self-interest. Instead, he insisted that we need to be intentional about loving others and resisting our many temptations to put ourselves first. One way to love others is by *not* insisting on having our own way.

There are several ways to translate and interpret 1 Corinthians 13:5. To say that love "does not insist on its own way" is to say that love "is not self-seeking" (NIV). Love does not pursue selfish ambitions, or seek its own advantage at the expense of other people. Gordon Fee says that love "is not enamored with self-gain, self-justification, self-worth."[4] There are other phrases beginning with "self" that we could add to Fee's list. Love does not live for self-interest or self-advantage. It does not pursue self-gratification but practices self-denial instead.

This is a good place to distinguish among several different kinds of love, all of which we encounter in the New Testament. *Eros* is the love of desire. It is not a selfless love but one that longs to have something from someone else. This explains why mythology usually depicts *Eros* (or Cupid) as a hunter armed with a bow and arrows; its love is possessive. *Philia*, or brotherly love, is a family affection. Its love is based on a personal connection with people who belong to the same family, church, city, or nation. Then there is the specific kind of love that Paul addresses in 1 Corinthians 13, which is called *agape* and is sometimes translated "charity." *Agape* is a uniquely Christlike kind of love. Its affection is not based on romantic attachment like *eros*, or on family connection like *philia*, but has a purely selfless desire to bless other people.

Frankly, this was an area where the Corinthians struggled. They did not love one another with a selfless love but often insisted on their own way. They did this when they were having theological disagreements, such as their argument over idolatry (see 1 Corinthians 10). Then, when they celebrated the Lord's Supper, some church members were barging ahead without waiting for their brothers and sisters (1 Cor. 11:21–22). Something similar was happening in their worship services: some people kept on talking when it was someone else's turn to speak (1 Cor. 14:26–33). So, in chapter 10, Paul said to the Corinthians—using vocabulary nearly identical to chapter 13—"Let no one seek his own good, but the good of his neighbor" (v. 24). What always matters more than who goes first, or who gets the last word, or who is right or wrong about nonessential matters of Christian practice, is how we love other people.

By setting a bad example, the Corinthians give us some good ways to test our affections. When I am engaged in an argument, am I willing to let someone else be right? When resources are limited, is it my habit to let other people go first? When someone else has something to say, am I able to shut up and listen?

Unfortunately, most of us have as much trouble in these areas as the Corinthians did. Selfishness is so deeply ingrained in Western culture that many people see self-love as a virtue; putting our own needs first is a sign of mental health. In the words of one influential psychologist, our highest calling in life is to "take loving care of ourselves."[5]

Our lifelong love for ourselves is the one love affair that most of us never abandon. We see it in the way people pursue their careers, always trying to get ahead of someone else. We see it in the way they spend their money, using it for personal pleasure rather than the public good. We see it in the way they treat their families: neglecting their children (or else driving them relentlessly), abandoning their spouses, putting old people away. People live this way because they are in love with themselves. No one has said it any better than the actress Shirley MacLaine, who once told the *Washington Post*:

> The only sustaining love involvement is with yourself. . . . When you look back on your life and try to figure out where you've been and where you are going, when you look at your work, your love affairs, your marriages, your children, your pain, your happiness—when you examine all that closely, what you really find out is that the only person you really go to bed with is yourself. The only person you really dress is yourself. The only thing you have is working to the consummation of your own identity. And that's what I've been trying to do all my life.[6]

The apostle Paul took a rather different perspective not only in 1 Corinthians 13:5 but also in 2 Timothy 3:2, where he identified people falling in love with themselves as a sign of the coming judgment. For his own part, the apostle tried to live a different way. As he told the Corinthians, "I try to please everyone in everything I do, not seeking my own advantage, but that of many, that they may be saved" (1 Cor. 10:33). This was the key to Paul's philosophy of ministry and the secret of his success in evangelism. He was not living for himself but for others, and so rather than promoting his own interests, he was able to advance the gospel. We are called to live the same selfless way, for as Paul went on to say, "Be imitators of me, as I am of Christ" (1 Cor. 11:1).

IN THE GARDEN

Paul's exhortation to imitate Christ brings us back to the saving work and perfect example of Jesus, whose life is love itself. Every part of the love portrait in 1 Corinthians 13 comes to living color when we see it displayed in Jesus Christ. As we have seen, his love is the most patient and kind, the least envious and boastful, of all possible loves. It is also the least selfish of all loves and the most insistent on seeking the good of others. The "Gift-love" of God, writes C. S. Lewis, "desires what is simply best for the beloved."[7]

Jesus never insisted on having his own way but went the way that would lead to our salvation. This was the story of his entire life. In Philippians 2, when the apostle Paul said, "Let each of you look not only to his own interests, but also to the interests of others" (v. 4), he proceeded to trace the story of the incarnate Christ as the perfect example of how to live for others and not for ourselves. Jesus let go of his grasp on all the glories of heaven. The Son of God became a man, and although he was Lord, he embraced the calling of a servant. Rather than saving his life, he gave it away, humbling himself "to the point of death, even death on a cross" (v. 8). So if we ask at what point our Savior refused to insist on having his own way, the answer is "at every point!" He lived his entire life for others and not for himself.

Yet there is one particular moment in the biblical Gospels when Jesus faced a deliberate decision as to whether or not he would go his own way. When confronted with this decision, he made the choice that only love makes. We see Jesus make this choice on holy ground, in the garden of Gethsemane.

It was the night before he died—the same night that he shared the Last Supper with his disciples, washing their feet and praying his hopeful prayer for the unity and purity of the church. Soon Jesus would be betrayed unto death. But before he went through with suffering and dying on the cross, he had a choice to make.

Matthew sets the stage, telling us that Jesus and his disciples went "to a place called Gethsemane" (Matt. 26:36). Gethsemane is the garden on the Mount of Olives that looks across to the city of Jerusalem. When they reached this secluded spot, Jesus said to his disciples, "Sit here, while I go over there and pray" (v. 36). Then he went farther into the garden, with Peter, James, and John.

This was no ordinary prayer meeting. Soon Jesus "began to be sorrowful and troubled" (v. 37)—words that indicate extreme emotion. He said to the disciples who were close to him, "My soul is very sorrowful, even to death; remain here, and watch with me" (v. 38).

In those agonizing moments of prayer, as Jesus was confronted with the terrible suffering that awaited him, we catch a glimpse of how much it cost our Lord to save us. Jesus was facing the pains of death by crucifixion, which by definition was an excruciating way to die. Even more, he was facing the psychic pain of separation from his Father. Soon he would take upon himself the weight of the guilt of the sins of humanity. As Jesus suffered this burden, his Father would forsake him, cursing and damning him to death.

The Puritan Richard Baxter thus concluded that our Savior's agony "was not from the fear of death, but from the deep sense of God's wrath against sin; which He as our sacrifice was to bear; in greater pain than mere dying."[8]

When Jesus said that his soul was sorrowful to the point of death, therefore, he was not exaggerating. In describing the same scene, Luke tells us that as Jesus prayed "his sweat became like great drops of blood falling down to the ground" (Luke 22:44). When Jesus said he was "sorrowful, even to death," it was as if to say that he almost died in Gethsemane before he went to Calvary. "In those supreme moments," wrote B. B. Warfield, "our Lord sounded the ultimate depths of human anguish. . . . In the presence of this mental anguish the physical tortures of the crucifixion retire into the background, and we may well believe that our Lord, though he died on the cross, yet died not of the cross, but of a broken heart, that is to say, of the strain of his mental suffering."[9]

YOUR WILL BE DONE

While he was under the strain of this supreme suffering, Jesus did what he had come to Gethsemane to do and started to pray: "And going a little farther he fell on his face and prayed, saying, 'My Father, if it be possible, let this cup pass from me; nevertheless, not as I will, but as you will'" (Matt. 26:39).

We do not know all the reasons why Jesus asked his Father if there might be some alternative to the cross, but the word "cup" gives us a clue. The Old Testament Scriptures mentioned two very different kinds of cups. One was a cup of blessing, such as the cup that "overflows" in Psalm 23, or "the cup of salvation" in Psalm 116. The other was a cup of cursing, such as the cup of wrath that Jerusalem drank in the days of the prophet Isaiah (Isa. 51:17), or the cup of judgment that Jeremiah prophesied for the nations (Jer. 25:15). This was the same cup that Jesus would drink down to the dregs: the bitter brew of the judgment of God.

It is not surprising, therefore, that Jesus asked if there might be some alternative. He was all alone. His closest disciples were too weak to stay awake with him and pray—even for one hour. Jesus was afraid—not sinfully afraid, of course, but naturally afraid of the pains of death and the suffering that would come from bearing the wrath of God against our sin. The physical pains of crucifixion would be as bad for him as they would be for anyone, but the spiritual and psychological terror would be even worse. Soon Jesus would be abandoned: the Father would see our sin upon the cross and turn away.

On the eve of his crucifixion, Jesus could have insisted on his own way. Given the choice, he would have preferred not to bear the weight of our sin, not to suffer the wrath of God, and not to be crucified on the cross. Nevertheless, the suffering Son surrendered his will to the Father, demonstrating the submission of love.

Jesus did this by praying the same way he taught us to pray: "Your will be done" (Matt. 6:10). Jesus prayed this way three times. First he prayed, "My Father, if it be possible, let this cup pass from me; nevertheless, not as I will, but as you will" (Matt. 26:39). His prayer in verse 42 is similar, but not identical: "My Father, if this cannot pass unless I drink it, your will be done." Later Matthew tells us that "he went away and prayed for the third time, saying the same words again" (v. 44).

The repetition of this petition makes it clear that Jesus really and truly did not wish to die. As far as his human will was concerned, he would have preferred some other way of salvation. Yet there was no other way. The only way to atone for our sins was by offering a perfect blood sacrifice. So Jesus surrendered to his Father's will. He did not insist on his own way but resolved the struggle of his human will in favor of his Father's pleasure.

We see our Savior's surrender in the progression of his prayer—there is not only repetition here but also progression. At first Jesus says, "If it be possible." But the second time he says, "If this cannot pass." The *if* in this instance may not be conditional. Indeed, sometimes *if* really means "since." For example, a child may say, "If it's time for me to go to bed, will you read me a story?" The *if* in that sentence means "since." So it was in the garden of Gethsemane, when Jesus said to his Father, in effect, "*Since* this cup cannot pass unless I drink it, your will be done." With these words he moved from wanting to explore the possibilities to seeing that there was only one thing to be done.

As we listen to Jesus pray, we cannot simply stand by as disinterested observers, because our salvation hangs in the balance. Jesus never would have made it to Calvary unless first he made it through Gethsemane. If he had never made it to Calvary, we would never make it to glory, which is exactly why Jesus prayed the way he did. Our Savior was committed to doing whatever it took to save us. Why? Because he loves us. According to Corinthians, what enables us not to insist on our own way is love. So when we see Jesus choosing to do his Father's will, we know that he is acting out of love. There is only one thing that chooses to give up its own rights, its own plans, its own comforts and desires, even its own life, and that is love like the love of Jesus.

PUTTING OTHERS FIRST

Now Jesus enables and empowers us to live with the same kind of love—love that does not insist on its own way, but puts other people first. John Calvin said, "It is very clear . . . that he lives the best and holiest life who lives and strives for himself as little as he can, and that no one lives in a worse or more evil manner than he who lives and strives for himself alone, and thinks about and seeks only his own advantage."[10]

Sadly, what Calvin called the "best and holiest life" is all too rare. Most of us strive for ourselves as much as we can, thinking about ourselves almost every waking moment and seeking our own advantage whenever we can get it. This is as true in the church as it is anywhere. When Paul commended the ministry of young pastor Timothy, he had to admit, sadly, "I have no one like him, who will be genuinely concerned for your welfare. For they all seek their own interests, not those of Jesus Christ" (Phil. 2:20–21).

To show the limits of our love, C. S. Lewis liked to quote the shortest review he had ever seen a critic give a work of literature. William Morris wrote a poem with the grand title "Love Is Enough." One critic responded with just two words: "It isn't."[11] The critic's point was that mere human love is never enough. People fall out of love every day. We find it hard to keep on loving people who do not love us back. We get worn out caring for people who have critical needs. Even when we try to love other people well, self-love keeps getting in the way.

Our self-love is like an oversized sofa bed that is too large for a studio apartment. No matter how many times we rearrange the furniture, the sofa bed is still too big. So it is with our self-love. Even when we try to put other people first, there is still too much of us getting in the way.

What we need is more of the love of Jesus. We need the love that Amy Carmichael asked for, as recorded in her dialogue with the word of Jesus through prayer:

> Beloved, let us love.
> Lord, what is love?
> Love is that which inspired My life, and led Me to My Cross, and
>   held Me on My Cross.
> Love is that which will make it thy joy to lay down thy life
>   for thy brethren.
> Lord, evermore give me this love.[12]

We can give to others only what we ourselves have received. Praise God, we are the recipients of an extravagant affection! The Son of God has set aside his own will to do the work of our salvation. Now, in the power and presence of his Spirit, we can show his love to others. In fact, this is what it means to love: to love is to be "toward others the way God in Christ has been toward us."[13] Jesus said this repeatedly: "This is my commandment, that you love one another as I have loved you" (John 15:12); "A new commandment I give to you, that you love one another: just as I have loved you, you also are to love one another" (John 13:34).

When Jesus called this a "new commandment," he was not saying that God had never before told his people to love. But he was saying that our call to love comes with new power—the power of his person and work. Jesus died on the cross to pay the price for all our selfish sins. Then he came back from the grave to conquer our sin forever. Now, on the basis of his crucifixion and resurrection, the Spirit of Jesus gives us the power to love.

Loving the way Jesus loves means being less insistent on having our own way and more consistent in putting other people first. We have countless opportunities to do this every day. Roommates can show love by what they decide to leave in the fridge, or by what they are careful not to leave on the kitchen counter. Children can show love by letting a brother or sister go first, by letting a friend decide what to play next, or by stopping whatever they are doing right away to go and do whatever their mom or dad wants them to do instead. Husbands and wives can show love by rearranging their lives to help one another. At the end of a long day at work, or a long day at home, are you mainly expecting your spouse to do something for you, or are you finding out what you can do for your spouse?

We practice the same kind of love in the church, or at least we ought to. We may have our own ideas about what ought to happen in ministry. But do we have enough love to recognize when we need to stop pushing and let someone else solve a problem their way instead of our way?

Not insisting on our own way has implications for what we do with our money and our property. In fact, one legitimate way to translate 1 Corinthians 13:5 is as follows: love "does not seek its own things." Yet this is exactly what most of us have: too many of our own things. By nearly every statistical measure, American Christians have more and more but are giving less and less.[14] Never before have so many had so much and yet given so little. What our stinginess represents is a failure to love. The less we insist on having things our way, and the more we put other people first, the less we will spend on ourselves and the more we will give to the ministry of the church, the needs of the poor, and the work of God's kingdom around the world. It is "the spirit of charity," said Jonathan Edwards, that disposes us "to forego and part with our own things, for the sake of others."[15]

Not insisting on our own way also has implications for the way we use our time, which may be our most precious resource of all. As you review your schedule, ask this question: How much of my time is dedicated to my own goals and ambitions, and how much of it is set aside to do something for someone else because I love that person more than I love myself?

As we try to love the way Jesus loves—not insisting on our own way—we should pray the way Jesus prayed: not "my will be done," but "your will be done." This was the kind of prayer that inspired Adelaide Pollard to write her famous hymn of surrender to God. In 1902 Pollard was hoping to go to Africa as a missionary but could not raise sufficient funds to make the trip. All her plans for her way of serving the Lord were ruined. In deep discouragement, she attended a prayer service where she overheard an old woman say, "It really doesn't matter what you do with us, Lord, just have your own way with our lives."[16] That night Pollard went home and wrote:

> Have thine own way, Lord! Have thine own way!
> Hold o'er my being absolute sway!
> Fill with thy Spirit till all shall see
> Christ only, always, living in me!

This is the heart's desire of anyone who wants to love the way Jesus loves: that he would live in us so completely that his love would flow through us and into the lives of other people. This will never happen as long as we keep insisting on having our own way, but only when we do what Jesus did and surrender our will to the Father.

9

LOVE BEARS ALL THINGS

Love bears all things, endures all things.
1 CORINTHIANS 13:7

*Then the soldiers of the governor took Jesus into the governor's
headquarters, . . . and they spit on him and took the reed and
struck him on the head. And when they had mocked him, they
stripped him of the robe and put his own clothes on him and led
him away to crucify him.*
MATTHEW 27:27, 30–31

As it says in the title of his best-selling spiritual autobiography,
the Romanian evangelist Richard Wurmbrand was *Tortured for
Christ*. Born a Jew, Wurmbrand gave his life to Jesus Christ in
his late twenties and began preaching the gospel a few years later,
when the Soviet Union occupied Romania and communism drove
Christianity underground.

Heedless of danger, Wurmbrand continued to preach the gospel.
Soon he was kidnapped by the secret police while he was on his way
to church and was put in prison, where he spent a total of fourteen
years in communist captivity. Over the long course of several incar-
cerations, Wurmbrand suffered many appalling deprivations. He was
mocked and beaten, burned and frozen, brainwashed and abused.
For hours on end the communists told him, "Nobody loves you
anymore, nobody loves you anymore, nobody loves you anymore."

Despite his many sufferings, Richard Wurmbrand refused to
give up his faith in the gospel, his hope in Jesus Christ, or his love
for the very communists who kept him under brutal captivity. What
enabled him to bear all this persecution and to endure all this suffer-

ing? Simply this: the love of Jesus. Here is what Wurmbrand wrote about what he called "defeating communism through the love spirit of Christ":

> In solitary confinement, we could not pray any more as before. We were unimaginably hungry; we had been doped until we became as idiots. We were as weak as skeletons. The Lord's Prayer was much too long for us. We could not concentrate enough to say it. My only prayer repeated again and again was "Jesus, I love Thee." And then, one glorious day I got the answer from Jesus: "You love me? Now I will show you how I love you." At once, I felt a flame in my heart which burned like the sun. . . . I knew the love of the One Who gave His life on the cross for us all.[1]

Wurmbrand observed the same love at work in the lives of fellow prisoners who also claimed to be followers of Christ:

> I have seen Christians in communist prisons with 50 pounds of chains on their feet, tortured with red-hot iron pokers, in whose throats spoonfuls of salt had been forced, being kept afterward without water, starving, whipped, suffering from cold, and praying with fervor for the communists. This is humanly inexplicable! It is the love of Christ, which was shed into our hearts.[2]

WHAT LOVE SUFFERS

The apostle Paul could give the same testimony, based on similar experiences of suffering for Christ. He too was put in prison for preaching the gospel. Paul was beaten and abused, mocked and tortured. Yet through it all he believed that it was a privilege to share in suffering for the sake of his Savior. The apostle never stopped living for Christ or loving people into the kingdom of God. So what he wrote to the Corinthians was truth he had tested by his own experience: "Love bears all things" and "endures all things" (1 Cor. 13:7).

These words come near the end of Paul's portrait of love in the Love Chapter of the Bible. The apostle started in verses 1 through 3 by declaring that we are nothing without love. He continued in verses 4 through 6 by listing some of the things that love does and does not do. Then in verse 7 he tells us what love is willing to suffer.

The word "bear" (Greek *stegei*) has generated a good deal of scholarly discussion, because there are several different ways to translate it. Here is how Charles Hodge explained two of the main possibilities: "This may either mean, bears in silence all annoyances and troubles, or *covers up all things*, in the sense of concealing or excusing the faults of others, instead of gladly disclosing them."[3]

Let us consider the second possibility first. The Greek word *stegei* can mean "to cover over" or "to keep hidden," since as a verb it is closely related to the noun for "roof." On this interpretation, the point would be that love knows when to keep things covered up or confidential. Although Peter did not use the same terminology, he expressed a similar idea when he wrote: "Above all, keep loving one another earnestly, since love covers a multitude of sins" (1 Pet. 4:8).

There are times, of course, when sin needs to be exposed publicly for the glory of God and for the real good of the person who has sinned. To give one famous example from the Bible, when Achan sinned after the battle of Jericho by stealing treasure that belonged to God, Joshua exposed his sin and gave him an opportunity to glorify God by making a public confession (see Joshua 7).

Yet there are also many times when love demands that we deal with sin more privately. It is at such times, writes Lewis Smedes, that "love has a fine sense for when to keep its mouth shut."[4] This explains why so much of the work of pastors and other spiritual leaders takes place behind closed doors. Love covers things up, not in order to conceal what ought to be revealed but to protect someone who needs time to heal; hence the rather loose translation in the New International Version: "Love always protects."

This is not the only way to translate the verse, however. The word *stegei* can also mean to support, in the sense of carrying a heavy load. On this interpretation, love supports other people in times of trouble. It is able to bear "all burdens, privation, trouble, hardship, toil occasioned by others."[5] When other people are struggling, love lifts them up the way that walls and beams support the roof of a building. This is certainly the kind of love that God has shown to us in Jesus Christ, who "has borne our griefs and carried our sorrows" (Isa. 53:4). Jesus has done the heavy lifting for our salvation. The Bible says that "he bore the sin of many" (v. 12), and that "he himself bore our sins in his body on the tree" (1 Pet. 2:24). Jesus has loved us by carrying the weight of our sin so that we can be forgiven.

Both of the meanings we have considered thus far are possible, but a third interpretation is the most likely of all. It takes the Greek word *stegei* to mean "bear" in the sense of suffering patiently all the troubles that come from dealing with other people, including people who try to harm us. It is one thing to come alongside people in order to help carry their burdens, as love certainly does. It is another thing—often a more difficult thing—to deal patiently with all the hurts that come our way when people attack us. Yet love is able to put up with anything and continue to love. It is willing, said Jonathan Edwards, "to undergo all sufferings for Christ's sake."[6]

This is the most likely translation because it is the way Paul uses the term *stegei* everywhere else, including earlier in 1 Corinthians. Back in chapter 9, as he explained and defended his ministry, Paul said, "We endure anything rather than put an obstacle in the way of the gospel of Christ" (v. 12). In saying this, Paul was not talking about carrying other people's burdens but about bearing reproach for the cause of Christ. Love is willing and able to bear all things for the sake of the gospel.

What Paul says at the end of 1 Corinthians 13:7 is similar: love "endures all things." Is there any real difference between "bearing all things" and "enduring all things"? The ideas are closely related, but if there is a difference, maybe Charles Hodge was right when he said that bearing all things relates "to annoyances and troubles," whereas enduring all things relates "to suffering and persecutions."[7]

Hodge also pointed out that the word for endurance—the Greek verb *hypomenei*—is a military term that means "to stand fast against the assault of an enemy." The person with this kind of love is able to sustain "the assaults of suffering or persecution, in the sense of bearing up under them, and enduring them patiently."[8] Many commentators have pointed out that such endurance is not merely passive but also requires active courage. It is "not a patient, resigned acquiescence, but an active, positive fortitude. It is the endurance of the soldier who in the thick of the battle is undismayed."[9] It is "the power to live vigorously if not victoriously in the face of evil."[10]

This kind of endurance shows up elsewhere in the New Testament epistles, typically in the context of persecution that can be endured only with great courage. In his next letter to the Corinthians, Paul would write of his own endurance "in afflictions, hardships, calamities, beatings, imprisonments, riots, labors, sleepless nights, hunger" (2 Cor. 6:4–5). But he would also tell them how he was able to endure: by "the Holy Spirit" and by "genuine love" (v. 6). Yes, it is love that enables us to endure: love for God and for our enemies, who will never come to Christ unless we show them his love. As Paul later wrote to Timothy, in explaining why he never gave in or gave up, but kept serving the Lord to the end of his days: "I endure everything for the sake of the elect, that they also may obtain the salvation that is in Christ Jesus with eternal glory" (2 Tim. 2:10).

For the sake of the gospel, love always endures. It "will not fail," said Jonathan Edwards, "but will continue. . . . Whatever assaults may be made upon it, yet it still remains and endures, and does not cease, but bears up, and bears onward with constancy and perseverance and patience, notwithstanding them all."[11]

THE SUFFERING SAVIOR

There never has been and never will be a clearer or more compelling example of love's endurance than the love that Jesus showed as he went to the cross. Since 1 Corinthians 13 is so often read at weddings, many people associate the passage with marriage. Yet the more we study what these verses teach about love, the clearer it becomes that they are really about death and sacrifice. The dominant image to associate with these verses is not the wedding gown but the cross.[12] When John Chrysostom preached from 1 Corinthians 13:7, he said that "love bears all things, whether they are burdensome or grievous, whether insults, lashes or even death."[13] These are the very things that Jesus suffered for us on his way to the cross and on the cross itself, where he gave his life for the sins of the world.

From a certain perspective, the whole life of Christ was marked by suffering: his descent from glory, his birth in a makeshift barn, his exile in Egypt, the attempted homicide in his own hometown, and then his homeless wanderings on earth. At last his weary steps brought him to the garden of Gethsemane, where in bloody sweat he agonized over his coming crucifixion.

Jesus suffered his entire life, but the greatest horrors were reserved for the last night of his mortal life and the day that he died. While he was praying in the garden with his sleeping disciples, Jesus was betrayed with a kiss. Though it was the middle of the night, the temple police dragged him before the high priest to face his Jewish trial. There he was falsely accused and wrongfully convicted on the charge of blasphemy.

Then, at the first light of dawn, Jesus was hauled before Pontius Pilate, the Roman governor. As far as Pilate could tell, Jesus was innocent. Yet the Jews kept clamoring for a conviction, so the governor sent him to King Herod, who had jurisdiction over Galilee. Before Pilate knew it, Jesus was back at his palace. Everyone was shouting, "Crucify! Crucify!" Finally, the governor gave in:

> So when Pilate saw that he was gaining nothing, but rather that a riot was beginning, he took water and washed his hands before the crowd, saying, "I am innocent of this man's blood; see to it yourselves." And all the people answered, "His blood be on us and on

our children!" Then he released for them Barabbas, and having
scourged Jesus, delivered him to be crucified. (Matt. 27:24–26)

Few things cause greater suffering than the unjust condemnation
of an innocent man. Yet this is only part of what our Savior had to
bear, what his love was forced to endure for our salvation. Even his
judge knew that he was completely innocent. Nevertheless, Jesus
was convicted of a capital offense and condemned to die.

Over the course of his several trials, Jesus was subjected to physical torture. Matthew tells us that Pilate had him scourged. Perhaps
the governor hoped to placate the Jewish leaders by torturing Jesus
instead of killing him. If so, then the Roman scourge was an ideal
instrument of abuse, a cruel (if not unusual) punishment. Pieces of
metal or bone were knotted to leather thongs and then flayed across
a prisoner's back. The torture was so severe that some prisoners died
before they could be crucified.[14]

What had happened to Jesus to this point was such a complete
miscarriage of justice that it is hard to find words adequate to
describe the horror of what he suffered. Yet what happened next
was even worse: Jesus was publicly, verbally, emotionally, and
physically abused by an entire battalion of soldiers.

When I was a child, I often looked through a book of paintings
that depicted the life of Christ. One masterpiece held a terrible fas-
cination for me: a grotesque painting by Hieronymus Bosch entitled
Christ Mocked (Crowning with Thorns). The men around Bosch's
Christ have cruel expressions on their faces. A soldier with an iron
fist holds a spiky crown, which he is about to press down on Jesus's
innocent head. A wizened old man looks up at the Savior with greedy
eyes, eager to see him suffer. Another man grabs at the folds of his
robe, ready to strip him naked. With oil on wood, Bosch sought to
convey the ugly scene that Matthew described in his Gospel:

> Then the soldiers of the governor took Jesus into the governor's
> headquarters, and they gathered the whole battalion before him.

And they stripped him and put a scarlet robe on him, and twisting together a crown of thorns, they put it on his head and put a reed in his right hand. And kneeling before him, they mocked him, saying, "Hail, King of the Jews!" And they spit on him and took the reed and struck him on the head. (vv. 27–30)

In order to understand what the Son of God lovingly endured for our salvation, it is necessary to linger over some of these details. The whole situation was designed to intimidate and degrade the prisoner by subjecting him to physical abuse and public ridicule. By the time the whole battalion had gathered, the soldiers knew that they were in for what they called "fun."

First they stripped Jesus, leaving him totally exposed. In the naked flesh of his genuine humanity, the Son of God was left completely vulnerable to physical pain. Strike his flesh, and it would bruise. Pierce his head, and it would bleed. Add to this the emotional anguish of standing naked before a leering mob.

Then the soldiers began to mock Jesus, making sport of his claim to be the king. A king should wear a crown, so they seized some thorns and fashioned a makeshift diadem. Pressing it down on his head, they drew blood from his kingly brow. A king should have a robe, so they covered him in scarlet. A king should hold a scepter, so they put a long stick in his right hand. A king should have subjects to rule, so the soldiers knelt down in mock homage and said, "Hail, King of the Jews!"

Thus the soldiers ridiculed Jesus for being who he actually was: the king of Israel. This is the bully's cruelest tactic. When a freshman gets hazed for being a freshman, when a band member gets bullied for being in the band, when someone short or fat or disabled gets teased for being short or fat or disabled, there is no defense. To get ridiculed for being who you are is to be left without any recourse, except to suffer more abuse.

The mockery that Jesus received was not limited to his kingly ministry, however. As we follow the course of his sufferings, we see him ridiculed for almost every central aspect of his person and work. Jesus was mocked as prophet. When he was in Jewish custody, the prison guards blindfolded him, punched him, and then said, "Prophesy! Who is it that struck you?" (Luke 22:64). Later he was mocked for his sonship to the Father. His tormentors said, "If you are the Son of God, come down from the cross" (Matt. 27:40). Then they mocked him for his miracles and his saving power. "He saved others," the religious leaders said, but "he cannot save himself" (v. 42). They even mocked him for his faith: "He trusts in God; let God deliver him now, if he desires him" (v. 43).

These were all reasons for Jesus to be exalted, not humiliated! Jesus is the King of all kings, the prophet of the Most High God, the miracle worker, the Son of God, the Savior. Yet rather than being praised for his kingly majesty and saving power, the true Son of God suffered the cruel taunts of wicked men. When we ourselves are verbally abused, therefore, we should never imagine that no one can understand what we have been through. Jesus understands. The Man of Sorrows endured the same kind of suffering on his way to the cross.

The next stage was spitting. Have you ever had anyone spit in your face? Spitting is a universal sign of contempt. It is one of the most disgusting, degrading, and disrespectful acts that one person can commit against another. Yet that is exactly the way the Son of God was treated when he became a man. Charge this to our account, along with all of the other heinous sins of the human race: we spit in Jesus's face.

But that is not all. Eventually Pilate's soldiers tired of mere verbal abuse and their mock coronation turned violent. This is characteristic of abusive behavior: unless someone intervenes, it gets increasingly hurtful until finally it becomes life threatening. So the soldiers took the stick they had given to Jesus—his makeshift scepter—and started beating him over the head with it. These men were brutal, sadistic, and inhumane.

SUFFERING SHAME WITHOUT SIN

Can you see the royal Son of God standing before the cruel soldiers in his scarlet robe with a crown on his head and the blood and spittle on his face? Even this was not the worst of it, however, for "when they had mocked him, they stripped him of the robe and put his own clothes on him and led him away to crucify him" (v. 31).

Everything else that Jesus suffered was only a prelude to his greatest suffering, which he endured on the cross. Crucifixion was a painful way to die—one of the cruelest forms of execution ever devised. Nails were pounded into the Savior's hands and feet. Then the rough wooden cross was lifted up and dropped into the ground. Jesus hung there until his lungs were crushed and his lifeblood drained out of his body.

Crucifixion was also a shameful way to die. Victims of the cross were crucified naked to show that society held them in contempt. But the law of God said something even worse, as any devout Jew would have known. According to Deuteronomy, anyone who hangs on a tree is cursed by God (21:22–23; see also Gal. 3:13). This was the curse that Jesus experienced on the cross when he was forsaken by his Father. It was the curse of the judgment of God, which he endured for our salvation. In the words of a classic hymn by Philip Bliss, "Bearing shame and scoffing rude, in my place condemned he stood, sealed my pardon with his blood: Hallelujah! What a Savior!"

Jesus bore the pain and the shame of his crucifixion with noble courage. The Scripture says that he "endured the cross, despising the shame" and bore "the reproach" (Heb. 12:2; 13:13). Jesus did not simply suffer these things but boldly endured them, going all the way to death without sinning or complaining. As it was foretold in the prophet Isaiah, "He was oppressed, and he was afflicted, yet he opened not his mouth" (53:7). So it was confirmed by the apostle Peter: "He committed no sin, neither was deceit found in his mouth. When he was reviled, he did not revile in return; when he suffered, he did not threaten" (1 Pet. 2:22–23).

The obedience of our Lord to endure all these things without sin is sweetly conveyed in the words of an African-American spiritual:

> Dey crucified my Lord,
> An' he never said a mumbalin' word.
> Dey crucified my Lord,
> An' he never said a mumbalin' word.
> Not a word—not a word—not a word.[15]

The silence of Jesus was essential, because in order to atone for our sins he had to offer a perfect sacrifice. Thus his uncomplaining endurance was a necessary part of the obedience to God that he offered for our salvation. It was also the proof of his love. Why did Jesus suffer the pain and shame of the cross? He did it because he loves us. It must have been for love, because the Bible says there is only one thing in the whole world that has the power to bear all things and endure all things, as Jesus did, and that is the power of love.

ENDURING THE WAY JESUS ENDURES

If we are the recipients of the enduring love of the Son of God, how shall we respond?

We should respond in saving faith, first of all, believing in a personal way that when Jesus died on the cross, he did it for us as much as for anyone. We do not have to bear the guilt of our own sin, but by faith we may transfer that burden over to the Son of God, who "loved us and gave himself up for us" (Eph. 5:2). An exchange has taken place—the exchange of love—in which Jesus has given his life for our sins. Believe this, and by faith you will receive the free gift of everlasting life.

Second, we should respond in loving gratitude. To thank Jesus properly for our salvation, we need to include more than simply the cross. We need to include all the violence and abuse that he endured on his way to the cross: the stripping and the beating, the mocking and the spitting. Have you ever thanked Jesus explicitly for the royal humiliation he suffered on your behalf?

In her book *The Hiding Place*, Corrie ten Boom writes about the lesson in gospel gratitude that she and her sister Betsie learned when they were standing in line for their weekly medical inspection at a Nazi concentration camp:

> I had read a thousand times the story of Jesus' arrest—how soldiers had slapped Him, laughed at Him, flogged Him. Now such happenings had faces and voices.
>
> Fridays—the recurrent humiliation of medical inspection. . . . [Naked, we] had to maintain our erect, hands-at-sides position as we filed slowly past a phalanx of grinning guards. . . .
>
> But it was one of these mornings while we were waiting, shivering in the corridor, that yet another page in the Bible leapt into life for me.
>
> He hung naked on the cross.
>
> I had not known—I had not thought. . . . The paintings, the carved crucifixes showed at the least a scrap of cloth. But this, I suddenly knew, was the respect and reverence of the artist. But oh—at the time itself, *on that other Friday morning*—there had been no reverence. No more than I saw in the faces around us now.
>
> I leaned toward Betsie, ahead of me in line. Her shoulder blades stood out sharp and thin beneath her blue-mottled skin.
>
> "Betsie, they took *His* clothes too."
>
> Ahead of me I heard a little gasp. "Oh, Corrie. And I never thanked Him."[16]

As Betsie ten Boom instantly understood, to be truly grateful for the gift of our salvation means telling Jesus how thankful we are for his endurance. It is to say, "I love you, Jesus, for the beating and the bruising that you bore for my redemption. Thank you for the blood on your forehead, the spit on your face, and the undying love in your heart!"

Finally—and this may be the hardest part—we respond to the love of Jesus by loving other people the way that he loves. How could we ever bear persecution or endure oppression without the love of Jesus? If we are able to endure suffering for the cause of Christ, this is a clear sign that the grace of God the Holy Spirit is working in a powerful way, giving us the love of Jesus. The apostle Peter said that if we endure suffering for Jesus's sake, this is a gracious thing in the sight of God (1 Pet. 2:20).

This is not to say that all of us are called to lay down our lives the same way that Jesus did, or that it is wrong to protect ourselves in godly ways from sinful abuse. But it is to say that true love is able to bear many hardships and endure many sufferings for the love of Jesus. Peter went on to say this: "For to this you have been called, because Christ also suffered for you, leaving you an example, so that you might follow in his steps" (v. 21).

What is the situation in life where God is calling you to endurance? Some Christians find their calling to suffer under the oppression of a government that is hostile to the gospel. Some of us suffer at school, where we are mocked for following Christ. Some of us suffer at work, where people have complaining attitudes that are hard for us to bear or make snide remarks that are difficult to endure. Then there are all the problems we have in our families—with our parents, our spouses, our children, or in other close relationships. There are people who have harmed us. They have wounded us with hurtful words and battered us with painful blows, whether physical or psychological. How can we possibly bear to love them? Only the love of Jesus can empower us to keep on loving the people that it hurts for us to love.

People sometimes say, "I know that God will never give me more than I can bear." Actually, there are times when God *does* give us more than we think we can bear. Sooner or later, we all suffer unbearable losses, or face insoluble problems, or have to deal with impossible people. But although God may give us more than we can bear, he never gives us more than *he* can bear.

We are not alone. Jesus is with us—the Savior who suffered every kind of abuse up to and including death by torture. This does not lessen our pain, necessarily, or solve all our problems immediately, but it does mean that we do not have to bear all things or endure all things on our own. The love of Jesus will carry us through. The more we know his love—the love of our suffering, saving King—the more we are able to endure all things for him.

10

LOVE TRUSTS

Love believes all things.
1 CORINTHIANS 13:7

Then Jesus, calling out with a loud voice, said,
"Father, into your hands I commit my spirit!"
And having said this he breathed his last.
LUKE 23:46

Would you still trust God if . . . ?

Would you still trust God if you had to leave your family behind and travel halfway around the world in order to follow his call for your life? What if you followed that call and your plans for serving God failed? Would you still trust him then? What if you were abandoned and ended up all alone? And what if you had to die a miserable death? What then? Would you still trust God if you lost everything you had in life, including life itself?

On the seventh of September, 1850, seven British missionaries set sail from Liverpool. Under the leadership of Captain Allen Francis Gardiner—a decorated veteran of the Royal Navy—they were bound for Patagonia, at the southernmost tip of South America. They had six months of provisions and high hopes for the work of the gospel and the kingdom of God. Yet the trip ended in total failure. The natives were hostile. The climate was harsh and unforgiving. The resupply ship failed to arrive until it was much too late. So the missionaries died, one by one, of starvation.

The party's surgeon was Richard Williams, and when his body was later recovered, the search party also found his diary. The last page was a dying testimony to the doctor's undying faith in Jesus

Christ. Picture the man huddled up in the hull of his little boat, suffering from scurvy, and writing the following words as his last testament:

> Should anything prevent my ever adding to this, let my beloved ones at home rest assured that I was happy, beyond all expression, the night I wrote these lines, and would not have exchanged situations with any man living. Let them also be assured that my hopes were full and blooming with immortality, that Heaven and Love and Christ, which mean one and the same divine thing, were my soul; that the hope of glory filled my whole heart with joy and gladness; and that to me to live is Christ and to die is gain.[1]

Richard Williams trusted God, no matter what. No *if* in life or death would ever compel him to abandon his faith. Right to the very end, he believed in the love of God, the glory of Jesus Christ, and the hope of eternal life. His diary thus stands as a lasting testimony to the truth of 1 Corinthians 13:7: love always believes.

ALL THINGS, ALL WAYS

The English Standard Version offers this translation: "Love . . . believes all things." This does not mean that love will believe absolutely anything. Love is not so gullible that it will believe something that is logically impossible, or fraudulent to the faith, or against the holy will of God.

On the contrary, it is the person who does *not* love God who is the most likely to be taken in by spiritual falsehood. When people stop believing in the one true God, they do not believe in nothing at all but will believe almost anything! Still hoping for eternal life, they believe in reincarnation, for example, or cryonic preservation. Whether they think that they will return to life as a different person entirely, or that future scientists will be able to warm them back into existence, they believe in anything that gives them the hope of immortality. Or, to take another example, many atheists believe that science is the only way of knowing and that human beings do not have a soul—only chemicals in the brain. In believing this, they leave out so many other things besides matter that also bring meaning to life.

So what does the Bible mean when it says that "love believes all things"? Some commentators think this verse teaches us to love other people well enough to believe the best about them. This interpretation goes as far back as Augustine. Rather than simply accepting every word of malicious gossip that comes our way, we should protect the reputations of the people we are called to love, including our enemies. To say that love "believes all things," writes Leon Morris, is to say that love "is always ready to allow for circumstances, and to see the best in others."[2] Love gives people the benefit of the doubt. Rather than assuming the worst about them and reaching our own conclusions about their secret motives, love always tries to believe the best.

Lewis Smedes thus contrasts the lover with the cynic, who basically refuses to believe anything at all, but always suspects the worst about other people. When the cynic sees people do something selfless, he tends to think that they really are acting out of self-interest. Rather than taking the risk of being hurt or getting taken advantage of, the cynic holds back from truly loving other people. But 1 Corinthians 13:7 tells us to make ourselves more vulnerable and to be ready to believe in other people. According to Smedes, "Love is a believing power, an impulse that moves us to trust people."[3] The cynic warns us not to trust other people too much, but the lover would rather trust too much than too little and therefore believes everything that ought to be believed.

There is another way to take this verse, however, which is adopted by the majority of commentators. Rather than taking the word "all" (Greek *panta*) as a noun, meaning "all things," we can take it as an adverb, meaning "always."[4] This interpretation avoids any misunderstanding about what love does or does not believe. The verse is not about the object of love's faith (what it is that we believe); it is about the perseverance of love's faith (under what circumstances we will keep believing).

Love is able to continue believing through the most extreme situations of hardship and suffering. Gordon Fee says it like this: "Love has a tenacity in the present, buoyed by its absolute confidence in the future, that enables it to live in every kind of circumstance and continually to pour itself out in behalf of others."[5] There is no limit to love's believing. It "never loses faith."[6]

MY GOD!

We find the perfection of this love, and of all love, in the life of Jesus Christ. We have already learned that his love is humble and patient, hopeful and selfless. We have traced the love of Jesus over the course of his lifetime. We have witnessed it in his teaching and his miracles, in his conversations with ordinary people and his prayers to his Father in heaven. We have seen his loving heart in the way he surrendered his will to God in the garden of Gethsemane and then courageously and sinlessly suffered abuse on his way to the cross. We have observed his love on the cross itself, where he bore the pain and endured the shame of crucifixion for our salvation.

What we have not yet seen is the faith of Jesus's affections, the way that his love always trusts. Perhaps the best place to see this is in the crucifixion itself, when Jesus was at the absolute extremity of human suffering. So we look again at the cross, and listen to the dying words of the Son of God as a testimony of his faith in the Father.

The gospel accounts of the crucifixion are not overdramatized, but understated. Luke simply tells us that "when they came to the place that is called The Skull, there they crucified him" (Luke 23:33). Nothing needs to be said about the deadly pains of that barbarous act except what we have said already: from the standpoint of physical suffering, this was an excruciating way to die. In this respect, the death of Jesus could hardly be considered unique. Many men were crucified in the days of the Roman Empire. In fact, at least two other men were executed the same way on the same day, one on either side of Jesus.

What *was* unique, however, was the psychic torment that Jesus endured—the suffering of his soul. On the cross a spiritual transaction took place. By the will of God, and according to his own deliberate intention, Jesus the Son of God took upon himself the guilt of our transgressions. As the sacrificial victim of an atoning sacrifice, he bore our sin. For this reason, in the hours that he was hanging on the cross, the Son was separated from the Father.

Here we encounter a great mystery of sin and guilt, of judgment and sacrifice, and of the triune being of God. While he was slowly suffocating, Jesus quoted the psalmist and cried out, "My God, my God, why have you forsaken me?" (Matt. 27:46).

These words come from the opening verse of Psalm 22, in which David suffers the anguish of unanswered prayer under the imminent threat of death. By taking these words on his lips, Jesus was declaring that he was dying a God-forsaken death. From all eternity, God the Son had lived in unbroken fellowship with the Father. But when he took our sin upon his shoulders, he suffered the wrath and curse of divine judgment against human sin.

Part of that curse was the Son's separation from the Father. This psychological reality found a natural symbol in the darkness that fell over the face of the earth. Here is how Luke describes the dim miracle that served as an outward sign of spiritual separation from God: "It was now about the sixth hour, and there was darkness over the whole land until the ninth hour, while the sun's light failed" (Luke 23:44–45).

The crucifixion of Christ was a black death. For three long hours the sun refused to shine. Regardless of its material causes, the descent of this darkness demonstrated that Jesus was suffering God's curse against our sin. This was in fulfillment of an ancient prophecy, foretold by Zephaniah: "A day of wrath is that day, a day of distress and anguish, a day of ruin and devastation, a day of darkness and gloom, a day of clouds and thick darkness" (Zeph. 1:15). This darkness and gloom symbolized the wrath of God against our sin. Isaac Watts said it well in one of his crucifixion hymns:

> Well might the sun in darkness hide,
> And shut his glories in
> When Christ, the mighty Maker, died
> For man the creature's sin.

Near the end of those hours of darkness Jesus opened a window to his soul that lets us glimpse what he was suffering inside. This is the only time in the Bible that Jesus ever spoke to God without calling him "Father." All of his other prayers began the way he taught us to pray, with the word *Father*. Jesus prayed this way at the tomb of Lazarus, when he lifted his eyes to heaven and said, "Father, I thank you that you have heard me" (John 11:41). He prayed the same way after the Last Supper: "Father, the hour has come; glorify your Son that the Son may glorify you" (John 17:1).

But when Jesus was in extremis, while he was bearing the dead weight of our sin in the hour that he was dying on the cross, he cried out to his Father and called him "God." This was partly to fulfill Psalm 22, but it also revealed the rupture in their relationship, the separation between Father and Son as Jesus died a God-forsaken death.

THE FAITH OF JESUS

It is desperately difficult for someone who feels forsaken to keep trusting God. Anyone who has had the experience knows this. When God seems absent and you fear that he is not even there, it can be almost impossible to pray. When everything goes dark, it is only by faith—not by sight—that we are able to hold on to God.

So it was for Jesus on the cross. The sky was black. In his soul he felt forsaken by the Father. But his announcement of abandonment was not the last thing he said. After saying, "My God, my God, why have you forsaken me?" his dying words were: "Father, into your hands I commit my spirit!" (Luke 23:46). It was only then that Jesus breathed his last.

These words are another quotation from the Psalms. They come from Psalm 31, where David prayed that God would deliver him from all his enemies. "Into your hand I commit my spirit," David said, and then he expressed his complete confidence that God would save him: "You have redeemed me, O LORD, faithful God" (Ps. 31:5).

Luke tells us that Jesus cried out these words "with a loud voice" (Luke 23:46). This was not a timid and doubtful request, therefore, but a bold and confident petition. Indeed, it was a confession of the Savior's faith. Like David, Jesus believed in redemption. He had the kind of love described in 1 Corinthians 13:7: a love that always believes. The apostle Peter gave more explicit witness to this faith when he said that while Jesus was suffering for our sins, he "continued entrusting himself to him who judges justly" (1 Pet. 2:23). Even in the most desperate circumstances, at the very point of death, when he was forsaken by the Father and crushed by the damnable weight of divine judgment, Jesus still trusted his Father's love.

Consider some of the things that our Savior believed. First, *Jesus believed that God is there*. He had to believe this to pray at all. Even when he felt forsaken and could not sense God's presence, he believed that God was there to hear his prayer, and he interceded accordingly.

Second, *Jesus believed in God as Father*. As the eternal Son, he had known the Father since before the world began. But in the weakness of his humanity, while he was dying a God-forsaken death, he felt distant from the Father. Nevertheless, he prayed to God as his Father. Before, it was "My God, my God," but now it was "Father" again. This manner of address was a clear testimony to his faith in the Fatherhood of God.

Third, *Jesus believed in life after death*. In committing his spirit to the Father, he was declaring that death by crucifixion would not be the end for him because his soul would live on, immortal. By quoting Psalm 31, he expressed his confidence that God would do for him what he once did for David, and redeem his life from the grave. By faith Jesus believed that there is a life to come.

Fourth, *Jesus believed in the Father's love.* By putting his spirit into the safekeeping of the Father, he was placing everything that was dear to him into the Father's care. Jesus could only do this if he had full confidence in his Father's love. When he committed his spirit to the Father, Jesus the Son was counting on a loving relationship with the Father that would continue for all eternity.

Fifth, *Jesus believed that his death would atone for sin.* He did not say this in so many words, but this was the implication of his prayer. When he asked the Father to receive him, he was asking the Father to accept the sacrifice that he had made for our sins in dying on the cross. He was leaving his saving work in the hands of God, trusting that the Father would raise his body from the grave and grant forgiveness to all his people. With his dying words, Jesus expressed his full confidence that we would be saved.

When we see Jesus on the cross, we see a man showing us how to believe all things. What enabled him to believe all these things was love: love for his Father and love for us. It is not just faith that has the power to trust, but also love. When we have the kind of loving relationship Jesus had with his Father, we are able to trust all the way to death, and beyond. The Father had always declared that Jesus was his "beloved Son." The Son had said it himself, in praying to the Father: "You loved me before the foundation of the world" (John 17:24). And when it came time for him to die, it was this love that carried him through.

IN GOD'S HANDS

Do you have the kind of love that Paul talks about in 1 Corinthians 13—the believing-all-things love that Jesus demonstrated on the cross?

Having this kind of love starts with knowing how much God loves you. When Jesus testified to the Father's love in John 17—in his hopeful prayer for the unity of the church—he also prayed that we would know the Father's love. Jesus said that the Father loves us even as he loves his only Son. Think of it: God the Father loves you every bit as much as he loves his only beloved Son! And the Son himself prayed that we would know this love, that the Father's love for the Son would also live in us.

Knowing the Father's love strengthens our faith. Lewis Smedes was right when he said, "The deepest motive for believing is the awareness of being loved by God."[7] If we find it difficult to trust God, therefore, we need to go back to his Word and consider everything it says about his love. There we will read these life-changing words: "The Father himself loves you" (John 16:27). We will also see the proof of these words in the gift of God's Son, who came into this world to show us his love.

This is the way that God makes believers out of us: he gives us his love. The more we experience the Father's love, the more we will learn to trust him, even in times of extreme need and desperate helplessness. We will learn to pray in faith the way that Jesus did: "Father, into your hands I commit . . ."

In times of financial need, when we do not know where we will get the money we need to pay tuition, or meet the rent, or repair the car, or buy groceries, or cover the medical bills, or provide for our retirement, we pray, "Father, into your hands I commit my finances." We pray this way because we believe that in his love, God will provide what we need.

We pray the same way in our struggle against sin. We may feel defeated by some particular transgression—a repeated sin that the Devil tempts us to think we can never conquer. But the love of God persuades us to say, "Father, into your hands I commit my sanctification. By your love, deliver me from the Evil One and give me your power over this sin!"

This is the way we pray about our health (or the health of people we love): "Father, into your hands I commit this body, asking you to heal this illness and to comfort this soul in its struggle with physical pain." It is also the way we pray about our schoolwork: "Father, into your hands I commit the homework that I don't understand, the grades that I can't keep up, the class that I'm worried about failing."

We can pray this way about everything in life: "Father, into your hands I commit my marriage [or my singleness]." "Into your hands I commit my family, with all its problems." "Into your hands I commit my ministry—whatever way you want me to serve you." "Into your hands I commit the community you have called me to love, with all its problems." "Father, into your hands I commit my future, with all its hopes and fears."

And when, finally, we reach the end of life, we will be ready to make the same petition that Jesus made when the time came for him to die: "Father, into your hands I commit my spirit" (Luke 23:46). Many Christians have made these very words their dying prayer. The first to do it was probably Stephen. When that worthy deacon was martyred for his faith in Jesus Christ, he said, "Lord Jesus, receive my spirit" (Acts 7:59). A century later, when Bishop Polycarp was martyred, he died with the same words on his lips. There have been others: Martin Luther, Philipp Melanchthon, Jerome of Prague, John Hus. When Hus was condemned by the Council of Constance in 1415, the presiding bishop said, "And now we commit thy soul to the devil." To which Hus calmly replied, "I commit my spirit into thy hands, Lord Jesus Christ; unto thee I commend my spirit, which thou has redeemed."[8]

Another notable example is Lady Jane Grey (1536–1554), who was Queen of England for only sixteen days. Because she refused to renounce her faith in Christ, Lady Grey was condemned to be executed. Upon mounting the scaffold she addressed the spectators with the following words: "I die as a true Christian woman, and I look to be saved by no other means but only the mercy of God and the blood of his Son, Jesus Christ." Then she knelt and recited Psalm 51 as a confession of her sins. Her executioner was moved to kneel with her and ask her forgiveness, which she willingly granted. Then she said, "I pray you, dispatch me quickly." Tying a handkerchief around her eyes, she felt for the block and laid her head down with the words, "Lord, into your hands I commend my spirit." Lady Jane Grey was only seventeen years old.[9]

Most of us will die less dramatically. But we will die (unless Jesus comes first), and when we do, we will need all the faith we can get. We will need faith to know that as we pass from this life to the next, trusting in the death that Jesus died for our sins, we too will pass into the loving hands of a loving Father who is waiting to receive us with open arms. Believing this, we will be able to pray, "Father, into your hands I commit my spirit."

Alan Paton prayed this way when his dear wife Dorrie was dying after a long struggle with emphysema. As he shared in his wife's life-and-death struggle, the South African novelist wrote an expanded version of the prayer Jesus made from the cross:

> Lord, give me grace to die in Thy will.
> Prepare me for whatever place or condition awaits me.
> Let me die true to those things I believe to be true,
> And suffer me not through any fear of death to fall from thee.
>   Lord, give me grace to live in Thy will also.
> Help me to master any fear, any desire, that prevents me from
>   living in Thy will.
> Make me, O Lord, the instrument of Thy peace,
>   That I may know eternal life.
> Into Thy hands I commend my spirit.[10]

It takes faith to pray this way. The way to grow in this faith is to know more of the love of Jesus, who not only showed us how to live but also showed us how to die. When you know the love of Jesus, you will trust him for everything: everything in life, everything at death, and everything for the life to come.

11

LOVE FORGIVES

Love is not resentful.
1 CORINTHIANS 13:5

He said to him the third time, "Simon, son of John, do you love me?" Peter was grieved because he said to him the third time, "Do you love me?" and he said to him, "Lord, you know everything; you know that I love you." Jesus said to him, "Feed my sheep."
JOHN 21:17

How delicious it feels to crave revenge! Although it is morally perverse and ultimately unsatisfying, the sheer pleasure that comes from nursing a grudge is intense. When somebody does us wrong, our anger smolders, and, to tell the truth, we enjoy the feeling. In fact, some people feed off their resentment for an entire lifetime. They say, "I will never forget what that person did to me!" and they never do, because as much as they hate what happened to them, they still love the taste of licking their wounds.

Who is the person you find it the hardest to forgive? Have you let go of every grudge, or are you still holding something against someone? If you have an appetite for revenge—if you enjoy the bittersweet tang of an old resentment—you need to know that in addition to making you guilty before God, failing to forgive will eat you up inside.

Doctors Daniel Amen, Marian Diamond, and Caroline Leaf have described what vengeful feelings do to the human brain. Based on biochemical research, these neuroscientists have documented the toxic chemical flood that our bodies release into our brains whenever we think malicious thoughts. Their microphotographs show how the chemicals that are released burn tunnels into the branches of our nerve cells.[1]

Dr. Leaf calls these burned-out neurons "emotional black holes." They are empty spaces in the brain produced by the angry resentments of a bitter soul. Yet, amazingly, it is possible for the brain to grow nerve fibers that fill in these black holes. New memories can replace the old. And one of the virtues Dr. Leaf identifies as bringing the most healing is forgiveness.[2]

GETTING RID OF RESENTMENT

The apostle Paul testifies to the power of forgiveness in his portrait of love, where he tells us that love "is not . . . resentful" (1 Cor. 13:5). Or, to express the same truth in a positive way, love forgives.

The old King James translation reads: "Love thinketh no evil." This way of stating things gives the impression that Paul is telling us not to think bad thoughts about other people. Love is not sinfully suspicious. If this is true, then the reason we have such a negative attitude about some people must be that we do not love them. In the words of Jonathan Edwards, love "is contrary to a disposition to think or judge uncharitably of others."[3]

Other commentators see a verbal similarity between 1 Corinthians 13:5 and a verse from the Old Testament prophet Zechariah, who said, "Do not devise evil in your hearts against one another" (8:17). It is certainly true that love is not devious; it does not draw up evil schemes against other people. Yet a careful study of the terminology in 1 Corinthians 13:5 reveals that it is not thinking evil or devising evil that Paul is warning the Corinthians about. His concern is not the evil that we are thinking about doing to others; rather, his concern is how we think about the evil that others have done to us.

The Greek verb that Paul uses in 1 Corinthians 13:5 (*logizomai*) is relatively common throughout his writings. It comes from the world of business—specifically, the field of accounting. It means "to reckon" or "to put to one's account." For example, in his second letter to the Corinthians, Paul declared that "in Christ God was reconciling the world to himself, not counting their trespasses against them" (5:19). In balancing our spiritual books, God has decided not to count our sins against us, but has reckoned instead that they were paid for on the cross. To say it the way a theologian would say it, God has imputed our sin to his Son, taking it from us and putting it over to the account of Jesus Christ.

In addition to not counting our sins *against* us, God has also decided to count the righteousness of Christ *for* us. Paul uses the same verb to describe this transaction in Romans, where righteousness is reckoned to Abraham and to us on the basis of faith (e.g., Rom. 3:28; 4:3, 5). So the idea of putting something to someone's account helps to explain both the doctrine of the atonement and the doctrine of justification—the payment of our sins on the cross and the free gift of the imputed righteousness of Jesus Christ.

When we turn to 1 Corinthians 13:5, we find the same verb used for an accounting of evil. Literally, love "does not reckon the evil," meaning that love does not "put evil to someone's account." The idea is not that love ignores evil altogether, as if it did not even exist. The idea rather is that love refuses to count that evil against people. According to David Garland, "The image is of keeping records of wrongs with a view to paying back injury."[4] Here the New International Version has perhaps the best translation, because it uses a term from the field of accounting: love "keeps no record of wrongs."

In other words, love does not keep track of sin so that it can settle the score later. Instead, it offers forgiveness, which may be defined as "laying down our right to remain angry and giving up our claim to future repayment of the debt we have suffered."[5] Here is a more complete definition:

> A forgiving person is one who, out of a profound sense of being personally forgiven a great debt by God, is quick to ask forgiveness

> from another, who repudiates anger, bitterness and a desire for revenge to initiate a loving approach to whoever may have hurt him or her, and who offers to freely forgive and forget the injury caused, with the hope that reconciliation may be achieved.[6]

This is an area where we all struggle. When people do something to hurt us, we tend to remember it forever, and if we get the chance, we will do something back to them that is every bit as bad, if not a little bit worse. At the very least, we will remind them what they did to us, holding it over them and using it against them. That way we can feel morally superior while at the same time excusing our own sin of being unwilling to forgive.

How hard it is to release an old resentment! Lewis Smedes defines resentment as "yesterday's irritation scratched into the sensitive membranes of our memory."[7] The scratches run deep, and in some cases they still bleed. People have betrayed our confidence or abused their authority over us. They have spoken hurtful words that we can never forget. They have damaged our health or injured our bodies. They have wasted our time, scorned our affections, or stolen our happiness. When these evil things happen, many people find it easier to hold on to the pain than to let it go. They refuse to give up the right to hurt someone else for hurting them. They keep replaying the wrong that they have suffered on the inward computer screens of their minds and hearts. Unless and until everything gets completely resolved and totally reconciled, they will never forgive.

When resentment builds this kind of wall, only love has the power to break through and release "memory's grip on yesterday's evil."[8] Love does not ignore iniquity but is painfully aware of whatever evil has been done. Nevertheless, rather than returning evil for evil, it seeks to overcome evil with good. Love "absorbs evil without calculating how to retaliate."[9]

What evil is God calling you to absorb? What memories is God inviting you to release? What person is he calling you to love? Is it a family member? A coworker? A classmate? A neighbor? A fellow member or leader of your local church? Rather than smoldering over an old resentment or longing for revenge, love has the power to make things new. As Lewis Smedes explains it, "Love lets the past die. It moves people to a new beginning *without* settling the past. Love does not have to clear up all misunderstandings. . . . Love prefers to tuck all the loose ends of past rights and wrongs in the bosom of forgiveness—and pushes us into a new start."[10]

In a word, love forgives.

PETER'S DOWNFALL

In connecting this aspect of love to the person and work of Jesus Christ, it is natural for us to turn again to the cross. In his dying hours Jesus pardoned the very men who mocked and crucified him. He said, "Father, forgive them" (Luke 23:34). In saying this, Jesus was showing us love's power to forgive. He was forgiving his enemies for their cruel betrayal, blind injustice, brutal torture, and cowardly abuse, not to mention their egregious evil in murdering the Son of God.

Yet there is another act of forgiveness that may hit even closer to home and touch us closer to heart. It was not just his enemies that Jesus forgave—including strangers who hardly knew him—but also his friends. Usually the deepest hurts come from the people who are closest to us, and for Jesus, this included his disciples. I refer specifically to Peter and to the time that Jesus forgave him.

Peter was the first and the boldest of the original twelve disciples. He was the first one that Jesus called to be a disciple, the first and only one to get out of the boat and walk on water, and the first to recognize that Jesus is "the Christ, the Son of the living God" (Matt. 16:16). He was the first to swear that he would follow Jesus all the way to death. Peter was first in discipleship, first in obedience, first in faith, and first in sacrifice.

Peter was also the first to fall away. The story is honestly and painfully told in all four of the biblical Gospels. After Jesus was arrested, Peter was brave enough to follow him to his trial before Caiaphas, the high priest. While he was waiting outside in the court-yard, a servant girl who was standing near the door said, "You also are not one of this man's disciples, are you?" (John 18:17). This unexpected question gave Peter a chance to stand for Christ at the hour of his greatest trial. Instead, he denied his discipleship. "I am not," he said.

Soon Peter found himself standing by the fire, where soldiers and servants were warming themselves on a chilly spring night. Naturally the conversation centered on Jesus. They said to Peter, "You also are not one of his disciples, are you?" (v. 25). Again Peter denied it. Before long he did it again, when another servant asked, "Did I not see you in the garden with him?" (v. 26). Peter replied by saying, "Man, I do not know what you are talking about" (Luke 22:60). Matthew adds the damning detail that in order to make his third denial more convincing, Peter called down curses on himself (Matt. 26:74).

To understand what it took for Peter to be forgiven for all of these denials, it is important to understand the nature and the extent of his sin. Usually we think of Peter as committing one sin three times, but in fact he was guilty of many sins, which he committed repeatedly.

Obviously, Peter was guilty of betrayal; he betrayed his commitment to Christ by denying that he had any relationship with Jesus at all. This was partly a sin of lying. Rather than saying what was true, Peter bore witness to something false. It was also a sin of profanity: by calling down curses, he was taking the name of the Son of God in vain. Add to this the sin of idolatry: Peter prized his own safety and security more than the worship of the one true God. His sin was also a failure to evangelize. Peter was so busy trying to save his own neck that he missed an opportunity to testify to the saving power and gracious mercy of Jesus Christ. We might even say that he was complicit to a murder, because rather than standing up for an innocent man when he was about to die, Peter refused to have anything to do with him.

All of this is exacerbated by the fact that Peter should have known better. What he did would have been bad enough for a recent convert, but Peter was one of Jesus's oldest and dearest disciples. Therefore, he could hardly plead that he was ignorant of what God required. On the contrary, he had often heard what Jesus said about telling the truth, worshiping God, and sharing the gospel. Because he had been so well instructed, God would hold him doubly or even triply responsible. Furthermore, Peter had been warned explicitly that he was in spiritual danger. Earlier the same night, Jesus had said to him, "Truly, truly, I say to you, the rooster will not crow till you have denied me three times" (John 13:38). Yet Peter went ahead and committed the very sin that he was warned not to commit. To make matters worse, the person that Peter denied was the very Son of God. There is a sense in which every sin is a sin against God, of course, but in this case that fact is especially undeniable. Peter sinned against God.

As we consider the precise nature and full extent of Peter's sin, we should recognize that there is more than a little Peter in all of us. Have you ever committed the same sin twice? Three times? Have you ever said something that wasn't true simply to make yourself look better in front of other people? Have you ever had a good opportunity to share the gospel but changed the subject because you were not sure what to say or how people would respond? Have you ever used bad language that included the abuse of God's name? And have you ever done these things even though you knew that you shouldn't? If so, then you have done what Peter did and denied your Savior.

PETER'S REPENTANCE AND FORGIVENESS

How do you suppose that Jesus should have responded to Peter? Many people—maybe most people—would have ended the relationship right there. If disciples were employees, Peter could have been fired for cause. After all, the man was unreliable, untrustworthy, and undependable. When you wanted him to stay on your side, he turned against you. When you needed him to stand firm, he fell down. So Jesus would have been fully justified in deciding that Peter was not worthy to be one of his disciples.

Jesus could say the same thing about every one of us, because we too have failed him in many ways. There have been sins that his Word warned us not to commit, but we went ahead and did them anyway. There were people we tried to love in his name, but we got so tired of dealing with them that we gave up. We had opportunities to take a stand for his gospel, but we chickened out instead. So when we see Peter fail, we also need to see how Jesus responded, because that will tell us whether there is any hope that our own sins will be forgiven.

What did Jesus do? The first thing he did was simply to look at his disciple. The very moment that Peter uttered his third and final denial, he heard the sound that froze his soul: the morning's first rooster. Peter had been warned that before the rooster crowed, he would deny Jesus three times. At that very moment—this is a detail that Luke carefully records in his Gospel—"the Lord turned and looked at Peter" (Luke 22:61). Luke does not tell us what expression Jesus had on his face, but we infer that he looked at Peter in love. Jesus knew exactly what his disciple had done. But rather than wanting to hurt Peter for it, he was starting to help him. The look that Jesus gave his disciple was a call to repentance.

Immediately Peter went outside and wept over what he had done. Were they tears of grief? Very likely they were, because his Lord was in the hands of evil men. Were they tears of confusion? Perhaps they were; who knew what would happen to Jesus? Were they tears of despair? Absolutely not! The disciple who died in despair was Judas, who regretted what he had done but never repented. Peter sinned against Jesus, too, but afterwards he repented for what he had done. His tears flowed from a heart that was truly sorry for sin. One loving glance from Jesus was all it took for him to know that he needed to repent.

Yet Jesus did more for Peter than simply call him to repent. A few hours later he went to the cross and paid the price for his disciple's sins. Jesus died for Peter and his triple denial as much as he died for any man's sin. This was the gospel that Peter preached for the rest of his life: there is forgiveness for the worst of sinners through the cross. Afterwards, Peter preached that Christ "suffered once for sins, the righteous for the unrighteous, that he might bring us to God" (1 Pet. 3:18). And when he referred to "the unrighteous," Peter was including himself as the disciple who denied Jesus the night before he was crucified. He knew that he was forgiven through the cross.

So are we. The forgiveness Peter received as a penitent sinner is the same forgiveness he preached for everyone. He proclaimed that Jesus had been crucified and killed by the hands of lawless men, before being raised up and exalted at the right hand of God (Acts 2:23, 32, 33). Then Peter urged that what we ought to do in response is exactly what he did: repent for the forgiveness of our sins (Acts 2:38).

PETER'S RESTORATION

When we do repent, we will receive what Peter received. No matter what we have done, we will be fully forgiven. We know this because what Jesus did for Peter on the cross—what he did for all of us—sets the stage for the remarkable reconciliation the two friends had after Jesus came back from the dead.

It happened on the shores of the Sea of Galilee. The disciples had decided to go fishing, with Peter leading the way, as usual. They fished all night but caught nothing until a stranger on the shore told them to cast their nets on the other side, whereupon they caught so many fish that they could not even lift them into the boat. As soon as Peter realized that the stranger was Jesus, he leaped out of the boat and swam to shore. This in itself is a clear indication of Peter's repentance. He was not moving away from Jesus but toward him, which is what we should always do when we know that we have sinned. We should not stay away from Jesus, as if we could deal with sin on our own, but instead we should go straight to the Savior for mercy, forgiveness, and grace.

Soon all the disciples were back on shore with their catch of the day. In loving service, Jesus had started a fire and prepared a delicious breakfast of bread and fish. Afterwards, Peter and Jesus had a heart-to-heart conversation on the lakefront, which for Peter was more like open-heart surgery.

It is worth noticing what Jesus did *not* say. He did not condemn Peter for his denials. He did not tell him that he was going to have to earn his way back into discipleship. He did not speak to Peter hurtfully or resentfully at all, the way most people would if they had been treated as badly by someone as Peter had treated Jesus.

The fact that Jesus did not say any of these things proved that Peter was forgiven, in the full and biblical sense of the word. Jesus was not keeping a permanent record of Peter's wrongs. He was not holding Peter's sin against him but instead was showing his nonresentful love. Rather than reckoning Peter's transgression against him, Jesus reckoned that Peter's account had been fully settled on the cross where he had died for Peter's sins.

As a result, Peter experienced the loving forgiveness that God shows to everyone who believes in him. He received the blessing of the man described in Psalm 32, "whose transgression is forgiven, whose sin is covered," and "against whom the LORD counts no iniquity" (Ps. 32:1, 2). Afterwards, Peter could offer the same testimony as the psalmist: "If you, O LORD, should mark iniquities, O Lord, who could stand? But with you there is forgiveness, that you may be feared" (Ps. 130:3–4).

So what *did* Jesus say to Peter? All he did was ask a simple question, "Do you love me?" and give a simple command, "Feed my sheep." Jesus asked this question not once or twice but three times. Clearly this was intended to remind Peter of his triple denial—not because Jesus was still holding that sin against him, but because he wanted Peter to experience the kind of forgiveness that would motivate him for ministry.

The first time Jesus asked the question, he said, "Simon, son of John, do you love me more than these?" (John 21:15). When he said "more than these," Jesus may well have been referring to the other disciples. Earlier Peter had tried to claim that even if the rest of the disciples abandoned Jesus, he would be faithful to the very end. What would he say now that he had failed to live up to his former boast? This time Peter refused to make any unwise comparisons but simply said, "Yes, Lord; you know that I love you" (v. 15).

Peter gave the same response a second time: "Yes, Lord; you know that I love you" (v. 16). But the third time was different. The Bible tells us that "Peter was grieved because he said to him the third time, 'Do you love me?'" (v. 17). Evidently Peter was grieved because three questions reminded him of three denials. Nevertheless, he remained steadfast in the profession of his love: "Lord, you know everything; you know that I love you" (v. 17). Peter was not afraid to say that for all his weakness, he really did love Jesus. He had the kind of love that grace compels.

This is what the love of Jesus can do for any one of us. First it takes our failures and forgives them. This gives us so much gratitude that we start loving Jesus in return. But that is not all. The love of Jesus then enables us to serve others with the same kind of love.

Peter was not simply forgiven and then forgotten, but he was also called into the service of love. Three times Jesus commanded him to take shepherding care of the people of God—in a word, to love them. "Feed my lambs," Jesus said (v. 15). "Tend my sheep" (v. 16). "Feed my sheep" (v. 17). Peter's failure did not disqualify him from serving the Lord. In fact, Jesus was entrusting to him his most precious possession: the blood-bought children of God. Peter was called to care for the sheep that Jesus loves, feeding them God's Word and watching over them in love, the way a good shepherd would.

FORGIVING THE WAY JESUS FORGIVES

Peter's restoration helps us to understand our own calling to love. Essentially, to "have love" is "to be toward others the way God in Christ has been toward us."[11] This includes offering them the same kind of forgiveness that we have received.

Loving the way Jesus loves always starts with understanding how much God has loved us. When it comes to forgiveness, we find that he does not count our sins against us, but forgives us through the cross of Christ. We have denied Jesus more times than Peter ever did, yet we are still forgiven. As Peter later wrote, "Love covers a multitude of sins" (1 Pet. 4:8).

When Peter said this, he was not thinking primarily of the forgiveness of our own sins but of the forgiveness we offer for the sins of others. Now we are called to love others with the same love as Jesus. Having been forgiven, we are called to forgive. Though we may not be called to serve as spiritual shepherds like Peter, we are all called to love. We are called to live out and to give out what we have graciously received: the love and the forgiveness of Jesus.

If we fail to forgive, then we fail to live out the implications of our own free forgiveness through the gospel. Amy Carmichael applied this principle to her discipleship with a series of conditional statements:

> If I have not compassion on my fellow-servant even as my Lord had pity on me, then I know nothing of Calvary love.

> If I know little of His pity, if I know little of His courage of hopefulness for the truly humble and penitent, then I know nothing of Calvary love.

If I cast up a confessed, repented, and forsaken sin against another, and allow my remembrance of that sin to color my thinking and feed my suspicions, then I know nothing of Calvary love.

If I take offense easily, if I am content to continue a cool unfriendliness, though friendship be possible, then I know nothing of Calvary love.

If I say, "Yes, I forgive, but I cannot forget," as though the God, who twice a day washes all the sands on all the shores of all the world, could not wash such memories from my mind, then I know nothing of Calvary love.[12]

By contrast, if we do have compassion, if we do show pity, if we do pursue reconciliation, if we do forgive and forget, then we are showing others the same kind of love that Jesus showed to us when he died for our sins at Calvary.

Are you learning how to love? Are you able to forgive? Or are you still burning with resentment for all the people who have "done you wrong"? Maybe you can relate to the words of John Newton, who by God's amazing grace was rescued from his sinful life as a slave trader. "So much forgiven," Newton said, but "so little, little love. So many mercies, so few returns. Such great privileges, and a life so sadly below them."[13]

Sadly, our love is not what it could be, and our forgiveness is not what it should be. Yet there is still hope for us in Jesus. We see this hope in the life of Kim Phuc. Though you may not recognize her name, you might recognize her picture. Kim Phuc is the naked nine-year-old girl in a famous photo from the Vietnam War of terrified people running away from a napalm attack near Saigon. Here is what she wrote about that attack, about its painful consequences and the grace of God that empowered her to forgive:

On June 8, 1972, I ran out from Cao Dai temple in my village, Trang Bang, South Vietnam. I saw an airplane getting lower and then four bombs falling down. I saw fire everywhere around me. Then I saw the fire over my body, especially on my left arm. My clothes had been burned off by fire.

I was 9 years old, but I still remember my thoughts at that moment: I would be ugly and people would treat me in a different way. My picture was taken in that moment on Road No. 1 from Saigon to Phnom Penh. After a soldier gave me some drink and poured water over my body, I lost my consciousness.

Several days after, I realized that I was in the hospital, where I spent 14 months and had 17 operations. It was a very difficult time for me when I went home from the hospital. Our house was destroyed; we lost everything and we just survived day by day. The anger inside me was like a hatred as high as a mountain. I hated my life. I hated all people who were normal because I was not normal. I really wanted to die many times.

I spent my daytime in the library to read a lot of religious books to find a purpose for my life. One of the books that I read was the Holy Bible. On Christmas 1982 I accepted Jesus Christ as my personal savior. It was an amazing turning point in my life. God helped me learn to forgive—the most difficult of all lessons. It didn't happen in a day and it wasn't easy. But I finally got it.

Forgiveness made me free from hatred. I still have many scars on my body and severe pain most days, but my heart is cleansed. Napalm is very powerful, but faith, forgiveness and love are much more powerful.

If that little girl in the picture can do it, ask yourself: Can you?[14]

Yes, by the grace of God, you *can* do it! You can receive forgiveness for your sins through Jesus Christ. Then his spirit will release you from resentment and give you his love, which has the power to forgive.

12

LOVE NEVER FAILS

Love never ends.
1 CORINTHIANS 13:8

For I am sure that neither death nor life, nor angels nor rulers,
nor things present nor things to come, nor powers, nor height nor
depth, nor anything else in all creation, will be able to separate us
from the love of God in Christ Jesus our Lord.
ROMANS 8:38–39

What is your experience with the love of Jesus? It is one thing to hear about his love but another thing to experience its power in your own life. So, have you found the love of Jesus and learned to live by it? Have you received it and started to share it?

For Augustine, who was one of the leading theologians of the early church, coming to faith in Jesus Christ was like falling in love after looking in all the wrong places. "Late it was that I loved you," Augustine lamented in his famous *Confessions*, writing about the years he wasted by running away from God: "Late it was that I loved you, beauty so ancient and so new, late I loved you! . . . I sought for you and in my ugliness I plunged into the beauties that you have made. You were with me, and I was not with you. Those outer beauties kept me far from you."[1]

How did Augustine ever find the love of Christ? Only by the grace of God, who reached out to him and saved him. Here is how Augustine described receiving the love of God: "You called, you cried out, you shattered my deafness: you flashed, you shone, you scattered my blindness: you breathed perfume, and I drew in my breath and I panted for you: I tasted, and I am hungry and thirsty: you touched me, and I burned for your peace."[2]

Not everyone would describe conversion quite the way that Augustine did, but what he captures so intensely is the way that the love of Jesus penetrates our physical senses. To know Jesus is to hear, see, taste, and be touched by his love.

EVERLASTING LOVE

One of the best ways to learn more of the love of Jesus is to study 1 Corinthians 13 in conjunction with the Gospels. In Matthew, Mark, Luke, and John we discover that everything the apostle Paul told the Corinthians about love is perfectly illustrated in the perfect life, atoning death, and glorious resurrection of Jesus Christ.

Jesus never does anything without love. Indeed, his love is everything the Love Chapter says that love should be. It is patient with sinners and kind to strangers. It does not envy or boast but offers itself in humble service. It does not insist on its own way but submits to the Father. It is able to forgive, trust, hope, and persevere.

In other words, the love of Jesus is everything that we are not. We illustrated this back at the very beginning of our studies in 1 Corinthians 13 by replacing the word "love" with our own names, and then substituting the name "Jesus" instead. When we insert our own names into the passage, we get awkward statements like "Philip is patient and kind," or "Philip endures all things." But when we try the name "Jesus," the whole passage reads beautifully: "Jesus is not arrogant or rude;" "He does not insist on his own way;" and so forth. Jesus Christ is the living perfection of love.

Nowhere is the contrast between our love and the love of Jesus more absolute than at the beginning of verse 8, where the Scripture says that love "never ends" or "never fails" (NIV). Were we to put our own names at the beginning of that verse, we would end up with a logical impossibility, because our own love often fails. But the verse is true for Jesus: his love never fails.

If we read 1 Corinthians 13:8 a little more literally, the verse says that "love never *falls*." According to David Garland, "There are different types of falls. Paul may mean that love never collapses in defeat, is never destroyed, never falls apart, never falls short, or never fails to have an effect."[3] True love never does any of these things; it never falls down. Yet it is evident from what follows that Paul is thinking primarily of the way that love keeps on going, not the way love holds together. The succeeding verses describe various gifts that will "cease" or "pass away" in contrast with love, which "never ends" but always "abides" (vv. 8, 10, 13).

To make this point, the apostle mentions several of the spiritual gifts that were causing controversy in Corinth because some people were making them the be-all and end-all of the Christian life. Paul's point is simply that however useful these gifts may be, they are temporary and transitory, and therefore they are not as important as love, which will last forever.

Take prophecy, for instance. Prophecy is one of the greatest of all spiritual gifts. When the prophet speaks, even the king must listen. But "as for prophecies," Paul says, "they will pass away" (v. 8). The prophet speaks in anticipation of what God will do. The Old Testament prophets looked forward to the coming of Christ. New Testament prophecy is about Christ coming again. But when he does come again, history will reach its end, and there will be no more need for any prophecy.

The same is true of tongues, which was another gift at the center of controversy in Corinth. Some church members seemed to think that by speaking the language of heaven, they were "already partakers of the ultimate state of spiritual existence."[4] Not so fast, the apostle said: "as for tongues, they will cease" (v. 8).

Even knowledge "will pass away" (v. 8)—not knowledge in the sense of grasping the truth, which will endure forever, but knowledge as a spiritual gift to understand mysteries that are presently beyond us, but one day will be revealed. This meaning is clear from what Paul says in the verses that follow: "For we know in part and we prophesy in part, but when the perfect comes, the partial will pass away" (vv. 9–10). One day Jesus will come to make all things perfect, and when that day comes, we will no longer need spiritual gifts—like knowledge and prophecy—which help us prepare for his coming. But we will still need love.

NOW AND THEN

Paul shows the difference between the way things are now and the way things will be when God makes everything perfect by using two analogies: a child and a mirror. "When I was a child," he says, "I spoke like a child, I thought like a child, I reasoned like a child. When I became a man, I gave up childish ways. For now we see in a mirror dimly, but then face to face. Now I know in part; then I shall know fully, even as I have been fully known" (vv. 11–12).

What a child understands about the world is true as far as it goes. But when it comes to understanding the way things work, there is a huge difference between childhood and adulthood. There is also a huge difference between seeing someone's reflection in a mirror and meeting someone in person. The city of Corinth produced some of the finest bronze mirrors in the ancient world.[5] But even the best mirror gives us only indirect perception; it is no substitute for having a real-life relationship and speaking with someone face-to-face.

Paul makes these comparisons to show that whatever knowledge we gain from whatever spiritual gifts we have is only partial in comparison to the perfect knowledge that we will have in eternity when we see Jesus face-to-face. When his perfection finally comes, everything that is not permanent will pass away. This includes the gifts of prophecy, knowledge, and tongues, which God has planned to make obsolete. So rather than making spiritual gifts our main priority, we should learn how to love, which is something that will last forever. Mark Dever expresses the thought beautifully: "Although prophecy and knowledge will pass away, love will remain, even in the rarified celestial atmosphere of the unmediated presence of God."[6]

What Paul says about spiritual gifts really is true of every earthly thing: it will all pass away. Even the world itself will be destroyed with fire (2 Pet. 3:7). But love will outlast everything. Divine affection will fill everything in "a new heaven and a new earth" (Rev. 21:1), including our own hearts and lives. "Then," wrote Jonathan Edwards, "in every heart, that love which now seems as but a spark, shall be kindled to a bright and glowing flame, and every ransomed soul shall be as it were in a blaze of divine and holy love, and shall remain and grow in this glorious perfection and blessedness through all eternity!"[7] Because God himself is love, love will go on forever.

It is the staying power of love, most of all, which explains the triumphant and climactic statement at the conclusion of the Love Chapter: "So now faith, hope, and love abide, these three; but the greatest of these is love" (1 Cor. 13:13). Love is superior even to the cardinal virtues of faith and hope. To quote the title of a famous old sermon on this passage, love is "the greatest thing in the world."[8] What makes it so great is that it will never end. According to Charles Hodge, love is "not designed and adapted merely to the present state of existence, but to our future and immortal state of being."[9] The durability of love is in a class by itself. It is not just for now; it is forever.

THE PROOF OF GOD'S LOVE

If 1 Corinthians 13 is a portrait of love, then it must be a portrait of Jesus Christ, who is love incarnate. Every aspect of love finds its perfection in his affection. To live out the Love Chapter is to learn how to love the way Jesus loves. Only his love is constantly patient and perfectly kind. Only his love never envies or boasts, but always puts other people first. Only his love never gets sinfully irritated or unrighteously angry, but always serves and always forgives. Only his love has the strength to bear all things, the faith to believe all things, and the perseverance to endure all things. Now we can add this to everything else that we have said about the love of Jesus: his love is all of these things . . . forever. The love of Jesus never, ever fails.

Where is the best place in the Bible to prove this? In his promise at the end of the Gospels, Jesus tells us that he will be with us "always, to the end of the age" (Matt. 28:20). But at the end of Romans 8 Paul extends this promise beyond the end of history to show that the love God has for us in Jesus will never end:

> If God is for us, who can be against us? He who did not spare his own Son but gave him up for us all, how will he not also with him graciously give us all things? Who shall bring any charge against God's elect? It is God who justifies. Who is to condemn? Christ Jesus is the one who died—more than that, who was raised—who is at the right hand of God, who indeed is interceding for us. Who shall separate us from the love of Christ? Shall tribulation, or distress, or persecution, or famine, or nakedness, or danger, or sword? As it is written, "For your sake we are being killed all the day long; we are regarded as sheep to be slaughtered." No, in all these things we are more than conquerors through him who loved us. For I am sure that neither death nor life, nor angels nor rulers, nor things present nor things to come, nor powers, nor height nor depth, nor anything else in all creation, will be able to separate us from the love of God in Christ Jesus our Lord. (vv. 31–39)

There are times in life when we are tempted to think that God has turned against us, or to fear that he will abandon us, or to worry that he might stop loving us. There are many reasons why we have these thoughts and fears. Sometimes our sufferings are so great that we cannot see how God could be loving at all. Sometimes the guilt of our sin makes God's love feel far away. Sometimes our fears get the best of us, and we worry about things that we know, deep down, are not true to the Word of God. But whenever we are tempted to doubt the love of God, the place to turn is to the end of Romans 8, where the apostle Paul makes a knock-down, drag-out argument to prove that nothing can ever separate us from the love of Jesus.

MORE THAN CONQUERORS

Paul begins by arguing from the greater to the lesser: "He who did not spare his own Son but gave him up for us all, how will he not also with him graciously give us all things?" (Rom. 8:32). Follow Paul's logic. God the Father has already given us the greatest gift in the world: his own Son to be our Savior. He did not spare the Son, but gave him through suffering and death for our salvation. If God loves us enough to give us his Son, the Scripture argues, then he will do any and every other loving thing for us that we will ever need— everything from adopting us as his children to taking us home to glory (vv. 29–30).

Yet we may still be tempted to doubt the love of God. So the apostle considers some of the things that might perhaps take away that love. In verses 33 and 34 he contemplates the possibility of legal troubles. Some people worry about being morally disqualified. Their sins are so sinful that if Satan (that clever prosecutor) were to show up one day and accuse them, they fear that they would be banished from the sight of God forever. But the Bible says no! If we trust in Jesus for the forgiveness of our sins, then God himself—the infinite and almighty God—will declare that we are righteous. Who, therefore, "shall bring any charge against God's elect? It is God who justifies" (v. 33).

Even if no one brings a legal charge against us, maybe we will still be condemned by the Judge himself. Paul responds to this doubt with a rhetorical question: "Who is to condemn?" The answer is "No one!" If God does not condemn us, then no one else can, because God rules the world. God has promised not to condemn us because we are covered by the righteousness of Jesus Christ. At this very moment, Jesus is praying—efficaciously—for our salvation. So Paul answers his own rhetorical question by saying, "Christ Jesus is the one who died—more than that, who was raised—who is at the right hand of God, who indeed is interceding for us" (v. 34). Who therefore can possibly condemn us if Jesus himself—who died for us and has been raised from the dead for our justification—is there to defend us against every criminal charge?

Next the apostle turns from legal troubles to the other troubles of life. Here is another unanswerable question: "Who shall separate us from the love of Christ? Shall tribulation, or distress, or persecution, or famine, or nakedness, or danger, or sword?" (v. 35). These are all serious dangers, as Paul well knew, because he had faced them himself. Here he describes the kinds of physical dangers that are common to humanity, but especially for the people of God as they do kingdom work and sometimes suffer for the cause of Christ. There is tribulation and persecution, poverty and hunger, war and violence—everything up to and including martyrdom. This has been the experience of God's people down through the ages. Paul proves this by reaching back to one of the psalms of David, where he sees the same kind of suffering: "For your sake we are being killed all the day long; we are regarded as sheep to be slaughtered" (v. 36).

When we ourselves suffer such troubles, it is tempting to think that God must not love us. Otherwise, we reason, he wouldn't be letting this happen to us! But the Bible insists that if we try to interpret God's affections on the basis of our present circumstances, we are bound to misconstrue his intentions. No matter what we are going through, God is loving us all the time. There is no trouble or hardship that truly separates us from the love of God. "No," the apostle says, "in all these things we are more than conquerors through him who loved us" (v. 37).

This has been the testimony of suffering, conquering believers down through the ages. By the grace of God and the work of the Holy Spirit, it will be our own testimony in all the hard struggles of life. When we are tempted to doubt the love of God, we need to preach the gospel to ourselves, saying, "My Father God has not spared to give me his own Son. My Lord Jesus Christ has sacrificed his life for my sins and even now is praying for my salvation. Therefore, by the work of his Spirit in my life nothing can ever, ever separate me from the love of God."

At the end of his life, when his body was old and weak, the Reformation theologian Caspar Olevianus was filled with faith in the love that God had for him in Jesus Christ. Even when his physical senses were almost too weak to perceive the world around him, Olevianus did not lose his grasp on the love of God. His dying testimony was, "My hearing is gone, my smelling is gone, and my sight is going: my speech and feeling are almost gone; but the loving-kindness of God is still the same, and will never depart from me."[10]

INVINCIBLE LOVE

Do you believe that the love of God will never leave you? The apostle Paul certainly did. He was absolutely convinced that his whole life—even with all its suffering—was under the love of God. So as his argument for the inescapable love of God built to its logical and rhetorical climax, he listed every obstacle that he could possibly imagine, and then he said that none of them could ever get in the way of God's love for us in Jesus. He said, "I am sure that neither death nor life, nor angels nor rulers, nor things present nor things to come, nor powers, nor height nor depth, nor anything else in all creation, will be able to separate us from the love of God in Christ Jesus our Lord" (vv. 38–39).

Paul starts with death, which elsewhere he calls "the last enemy" (1 Cor. 15:26). Death is the most fearful of all dividers because it has the power to separate us from the ones we love. But death cannot separate us from love itself, because for those who believe in Christ, death is a doorway to the presence of God. Our Savior Jesus Christ has "abolished death and brought life and immortality to light through the gospel" (2 Tim. 1:10). Therefore, death does not divide us from God's love but actually unites us to God and to his love forever. In the words of Alexander Maclaren, "The separator becomes the uniter; he rends us apart from the world that he may 'bring us to God.'"[11]

The inability of death to separate us from the love of God is illustrated by the testimony of a young pastor who was called to the bedside of an old woman who was at the end of her days. When he tried to comfort her by muttering something about how sorry he was that she was going to die, she interrupted him. "God bless you, young man," she said. "There's nothing to be scared about. I'm just going to cross over Jordan in a few hours, and my Father owns the land on both sides of the river."[12]

Death cannot separate us from the love of God, but what about life? If this seems like a strange question to ask, then you are indeed blessed, because many people know that life can be crueler than death. Yet the Scripture assures us that no matter what we suffer in life, God is still with us. Jesus knows what it is like to suffer, because he suffered himself, and in our suffering he continues to show us his love.

Having considered the great issues of life and death, Paul turns next to various authorities. He is convinced that neither "angels nor rulers" can separate us from the love of God. There is some debate as to whether "angels" refers to good angels or to bad angels, the demons who fell into sin with Satan and are always trying to trouble the people of God. In fact, the Greek word for "Devil" (*diabolos*) means "separator" or "divider." There is also some debate as to whether *rulers* refers to earthly or heavenly powers—to governments or to gods.

Whoever these rulers are, they cannot separate us from the love of God. The most that the demons can do—as powerful as they are—is tempt us to *think* that God does not love us. But they cannot keep God from actually loving us, as he always does. Earthly powers are even weaker. They can close down churches, order God out of the courtroom, and keep him out of public education, but they cannot stop him from loving his people, any more than closing the shutters or pulling down the shade can make the sun stop shining. The love of God is invincible against all "the powers that be."

Next Paul considers time and eternity. Neither "things present nor things to come" can ever separate us from the love of God. At present we have no end of problems. Concerning the future we feel all kinds of uncertainty. But Jesus Christ is the Lord of history. He is the ruler of both this life and the life to come. Therefore, from now until forever we are loved with an everlasting love.

So much for time—what some people call "the fourth dimension." In verse 39 Paul proceeds to address the second and third dimensions: "neither height nor depth." Here the apostle speaks in spatial terms to show that there is no place in the entire universe that is outside the love of God. No matter where we go, God is there (see also Ps. 139:7–10). This is what gives some people the courage to go to the most dangerous places in the world, including places where they do not have even one single friend, and share the gospel. The love of God is everywhere. So whenever we feel alone, we can say, "Lord Jesus, I feel alone, but I know that you are right here with me, in all your love."

Life and death, angels and demons, present and future, up and down—is there any dimension to God's love that Paul has neglected to mention? Apparently not, but just to make sure, he ends by saying "nor anything else in all creation." In other words, there is absolutely nothing that can ever separate us from "the love of God in Christ." "Creation" includes everything that exists except God himself, since he is the one who created everything in the first place. So if God is for us, there is nothing at all that can ever keep us from him. His love will never let us go. We are bound to the living God, wrote James Montgomery Boice, "by a gracious, unchanging, eternal, and indestructible love."[13]

This is a love to build your life on, from beginning to end. This is beautifully illustrated in the dying testimony of the Scottish covenanter Robert Bruce. On the morning of his death, Bruce sat down to breakfast with his family. Suddenly he called out, "Hold, daughter, hold. My Master is calling me." Bruce then asked for a Bible and opened it to Romans 8. His sight was failing, so he quoted the end of the chapter from memory. Like the apostle Paul, he testified that he was "persuaded that neither death nor life . . . nor anything else in all creation, will be able to separate us from the love of God that is in Christ Jesus our Lord." After reading these words to his family, Bruce asked for his finger to be placed on these very words from the Bible. Then he said, "God be with you, my children. I have breakfasted with you, and shall sup with my Lord Jesus this night. I die believing these words."[14]

Robert Bruce had found what every believer finds: the love of Jesus that lasts all through life will be there for us at the time of death and then go on and on for all eternity.

PURSUE LOVE!

Since we are loved this way, we are called to live this way—loving the way Jesus loves. God has not given us his love so that we can keep it to ourselves but to share it with others. Jesus said, "This is my commandment, that you love one another as I have loved you" (John 15:12). The more we know the inseparable, indivisible love of Jesus, the more his love will flow through our hearts and into the lives of others.

First Corinthians 13 closes with a simple command that should motivate and animate everything we have been learning about the love of Jesus. The command comes at the beginning of chapter 14, but really it serves as the practical conclusion to the Love Chapter. It is a command that every Christian should take to heart. The command is simply this: "Pursue love" (v. 1). To read the verse more literally, "Follow love," "Run for love," or even "Chase love." The Greek verb (*diokete*) describes someone who is going hard after love.

This clear command gives us a simple way to test our commitment to Christ. A Christian is someone who has experienced the love of Jesus and who therefore pursues love in relationship to other people. So the question is: Am I pursuing love? Am I going hard after love? Have I made love my lifelong pursuit? Jonathan Edwards said, "If love is so great a thing in Christianity, so essential and distinguishing, yea, the very sum of all Christian virtue, then surely those that profess themselves Christians should live in love, and abound in the works of love."[15]

Anyone who has read and studied 1 Corinthians 13 should have some idea what it would look like to live in the headlong pursuit of love. It means being patient with other people's failings. It means being kind to people, even when they don't seem to deserve it. It means not promoting ourselves, or boasting about our accomplishments, or insisting on having our own way. It means making less of ourselves and more of others. It means forgiving people when they hurt us and refusing to get angry with them when they irritate us. It means believing the best truth about other people, not the worst falsehood. It means that even in the most desperate circumstances, we are able to keep believing, keep hoping, and keep loving.

This is the high calling of the love of Jesus—a lifelong calling in which, of course, we all fail miserably. When we read that love never fails, we know immediately that we fall well short of God's perfection. We find it so hard to love other people that we give up long before God stops demanding our love or other people stop needing it. We get tired of running after love; our affections slow to a jog, then to a walk, before finally we give up the chase altogether. Our love often fails. Indeed, we fail to love as much as we fail at anything else in life.

It is when we run out of love, especially, that we need to remember the never-failing love of Jesus. When the Scripture says that nothing can separate us from the love of God, this includes our own feeble efforts to love like Jesus. As we try and often fail to love, we are at the very same time being loved by God, because we can never be separated from that love! Therefore, we should never say, "I have no love left to give," because at the very moment we say that, we are still being loved by the invincible love of Jesus. At every place in life where we find it hard to love, the love of Jesus is there to help us. Not even a loveless heart can separate us from his love. By faith in the Son of God, we are permanently connected to a love source that will never fail, and therefore our love can be renewed again.

So pursue love! Keep learning to love the way Jesus loves, recognizing this as a process that will take a lifetime. Live in hope for the day when, by the grace of God and the work of the Holy Spirit, you can write your own name into the Love Chapter with something less than total embarrassment: "Philip is patient and kind; Karen does not envy or boast; Julio is not arrogant or rude. Danielle does not insist on her own way; Jamal is not irritable or resentful; Renee does not rejoice at wrongdoing, but rejoices with the truth. David bears all things, Rosemary believes all things, Brian hopes all things, Elizabeth endures all things."

We are enabled and empowered to love this way because we are loved with an everlasting love. Jesus proved it on the cross, and he will keep proving it every day as we run hard after love. We will find, again and again, that we cannot love without his love to carry us along. But we will also find, again and again, that his love is right there with us.

As we look to Jesus in faith, we will give the same testimony that William Rees gave in an old Welsh hymn:

Here is love, vast as the ocean
Loving kindness as the flood
When the Prince of Life, our Ransom
Shed for us His precious blood.
Who His love will not remember?
Who can cease to sing His praise?
He can never be forgotten
Throughout Heav'n's eternal days.

STUDY GUIDE

CHAPTER 1: NOTHING WITHOUT LOVE

People talk about "puppy love," "falling in love" (or "out of love"), and losing our "loved ones." We even talk about "loving" ice cream or a particular house. Given the way we talk about love, it is hardly surprising that the word has lost its power. But a fresh look at 1 Corinthians 13 reminds us how beautiful Christlike love is.

1. Talk about a time when someone outside your family did something loving for you. What made that act or expression of love meaningful to you?

2. Read the familiar Love Chapter in 1 Corinthians 13:1–13. What might be different in your church if this chapter were applied primarily to love for other members of the body of Christ rather than to the love between spouses?

3. What distinguishes acts of mercy done without love from those that are motivated by love? Can the recipient or an observer tell the difference?

4. In 1 Corinthians 13:1, we are told that spiritual gifts offered without love are like a noisy gong or clanging cymbal. In what ways is a loveless Christian like a noisy gong? How would a person with faith and knowledge but without love come across to unbelievers?

5. One good illustration of Jesus's love for sinners is found in Mark 10. Read verses 17–27. What was the young man's motivation in asking Jesus how he could be saved? Support your answer with evidence from the text.

6. How can you see Jesus's love for the man in Mark 10:17–27?

7.   In Mark 10:17–27 Jesus responded to the man's question by telling him that he needed to love his neighbor. Ultimately, the young man failed the test of love because he was unwilling to sell all his possessions and give the money to the poor. Why was this man unable to give up what he had? Thinking more broadly, why is it especially difficult for wealthy people to enter the kingdom of God? What spiritual challenges do they face that poor people do not?

8.   In 1 Corinthians 13:3, we read that merely giving up our possessions to the poor is not enough. What else is needed? Why are good deeds insufficient without love?

9.   Think of the last time you were confronted by a stranger's needs. Did you pass the "love" test? If not, what stood in your way?

10.   What limits are you tempted to put on your love? What can you do to remove some of those limits and truly love your neighbor as yourself?

CHAPTER 2: LOVE THAT IS BETTER THAN LIFE

Some years ago there was a movement to encourage people to do "random acts of kindness" for strangers. In mind were simple things like paying for the person behind you in the drive-through—the kinds of things that would make another person smile. But the Bible's definition of lovingkindness goes much deeper. It is love in action for the spiritual benefit of others.

1.   How does today's culture define *love*? On what would the average person on the street base his confidence that his spouse or family members love him?

2.   Here is how the fourth-century preacher John Chrysostom defined showing kindness to those who have wronged us: "Not only by enduring nobly, but also by soothing and comforting" to "cure the sore and heal the wound" of a broken relationship. Share examples of how you have seen kindness heal broken relationships.

3.   Read Titus 2:1–15 and 3:1–3. Based on these verses, what problems were evident in Titus's church?

4.   Read Romans 2:4 and 11:22 and Titus 3:4–7. What are some characteristics of the biblical definition of kindness as expressed through Christ?

5.   How does the kindness of God affect us both short- and long-term, in the here and now and for eternity?

6.   According to Titus 3:4–7, why has God showered such kindness on us?

7.   Jesus told a story about what it looks like when we show kindness to others (Luke 10:30–37). What parts of this story would have been surprising or offensive to the expert in religious law to whom Jesus was speaking?

8.   What parallels can you find between the kindness of the good Samaritan (Luke 10:30–37) and the kindness God shows to us?

9.   What can we learn from Luke 10:30–37 about what it looks like to show true biblical kindness to another person? How does this differ from the world's definition of kindness?

10.   Think of the last time that you encountered a needy neighbor. Did you act more like the good Samaritan or like the priest and Levite? What motivated you or hindered you from showing or withholding kindness?

11.   Think of someone who may not seem to deserve your love—someone to whom you could show kindness this week. What kind act will you do for him or her in the name of Christ? Share your plan with someone who can keep you accountable for following through.

CHAPTER 3: LOVE IS NOT IRRITABLE

Think about the last time you were irritated with a loved one. You can probably recall exactly what he or she did to annoy you, but it may be harder to remember honestly how you responded. Perhaps you didn't think much about your response once the moment had passed. But the Bible holds us accountable for our irritability, even if we have a "really good reason" for our short temper. We often excuse our fits of anger by saying we were provoked or tired. But in the middle of 1 Corinthians 13 Paul reminds us that love and irritability are mutually exclusive. Our irritated outburst was, in fact, an act of hatred.

1. It is easy to get irritated with others, especially those who live or work or study in close proximity to us. What factors contribute to your being irritated with others?

2. Which of the definitions for irritability offered on pages 44–46 is most helpful to you and why? What further synonyms or examples of irritability would you add to complete those sentences: love is not_____ or love does not _____? *A way of hating.*

3. Read Mark 6:30–32. Jesus and the disciples were coming off a busy season of ministry. What were the disciples expecting and looking forward to? *Rest Send People Away*

4. Read Mark 6:33–37. Instead of enjoying a retreat, Jesus and his disciples were greeted by more needy crowds. What evidence do you see in these verses that the disciples were being irritable rather than loving? What factors may have contributed to their short tempers?

5. Read Mark 6:38–40. From a merely human perspective, what reasons would Jesus have had to be annoyed with the crowds? How did he respond instead?

6. After all the disciples had seen and experienced by living and working with Jesus, you would think they might have exhibited a bit more patience and compassion. But nowhere in Mark 6:30–40 did Jesus reprimand them for their short tempers. How did Jesus help the disciples get over their anger?

7. If you had been in the disciples' place, how would your attitude have changed from the beginning of this episode to the end?

8. What can we learn from Mark 6:38–40 about showing compassion in the midst of trying circumstances?

9. What practical strategies can you implement to help yourself be less irritable? How can you help to defuse stressful situations so that others keep their tempers in check also?

10. Describe a time when you or someone else exhibited irritability and then apologized afterward. When you have been short-tempered with someone, what can you say or do to reconcile the relationship?

CHAPTER 4: LOVE'S HOLY JOY

Life moves from one celebration to the next. Thanksgiving is followed by Christmas, then Valentine's Day, with birthdays and anniversaries thrown in to keep the party rolling.

It is wonderful to be able to celebrate with family and friends. But sometimes, in our heart of hearts, we rejoice at the wrong things. We're secretly delighted when someone gets passed over for a job or misses out on an award. Or we are glad so-and-so's "perfect" child didn't make the play, while our kid did. Or, worse, we celebrate sin. We are happy to witness the moral downfall of someone whose politics or theology we disagree with. Or we join in raucous revelry centered on promiscuity and self-indulgence. At those moments, we are rejoicing at wrongdoing, something true love never does.

1.   Describe a personal experience in which an occasion of celebration turned into something ungodly or evil. How did it make you feel?

2.   Give some examples of when a Christian might be tempted to "rejoice at wrongdoing." What heart attitudes do we exhibit if we rejoice on these occasions?

3.   When have you rejoiced in the truth? What were the circumstances, and what truths were you celebrating with godly joy?

4.   Read Luke 7:36–38. How would you describe this woman and her actions?

5.   Read Luke 7:39–50. The Pharisee provides a stark contrast to the woman. How did his actions show that he was every bit as sinful as the woman?

6.   The Pharisee in Luke's story thought that Jesus's response to the woman proved that he wasn't a prophet, when in fact the reverse was true—Jesus's response proved that he *was* a prophet. What evidence does this passage give that Jesus was God's true Prophet?

7.   In Luke 7:36–50 Jesus contrasts the puny love of the Pharisee with the extravagant love of the sinful woman. What had the Pharisee neglected to do for Jesus, and how did the woman make up for each neglected task? What virtues did she exhibit?

8.   What can we learn from this passage about rejoicing at wrongdoing and rejoicing with the truth?

9.   In what ways are you like the religious person in Luke's story, and in what ways are you like the sinner? Where do you most see a need for growth in your own response to God's great forgiveness?

10.   Think about how you respond to those who have committed "bigger" or more obvious sins than you have. Are you sympathetic toward their weakness or secretly glad that you "would never do something like that"? Describe a time when you responded in a godly way and a time when you didn't. As you consider your reaction toward people with more obvious sins, how can you do better at rejoicing with the truth?

11.   According to the story in Luke, where does love begin? How can you experience God's forgiveness more deeply so that you can love more deeply? What are some outward characteristics that will show that you really know you are no more righteous than anyone else?

CHAPTER 5: LOVE WAITS

When we are kids, we want to grow up. Once we are grown up, we want something more or something different—a better job, another degree, a family of our own, financial security. But God often makes us wait for what he wants us to have, and always with good reason. God's love for us is patient, and because he loves us so much, he also asks us to be patient for the sake of our greater good and his ultimate glory.

1.   What is your biggest pet peeve, the thing that makes you most impatient with your loved ones? How do you express your impatience (a dramatic sigh, raised voice, something else)?

2.   Read Romans 2:4; 1 Timothy 1:16; and 2 Peter 3:9. What do these verses tell us about God's patience?

3. Read John 11:1–16. What details in the beginning of the story point to the urgency of the situation? Why is it surprising that Jesus lingered two extra days before going to his sick friend? Why did he wait?

4. Jesus's response to the disciples' concern for his safety (John 11:9–10) is somewhat enigmatic. What do you think he meant?

5. Read John 11:17–44. What evidence do you see of Jesus's patient love?

6. What did Mary and Martha learn from this event in John's Gospel about Jesus and his love?

7. What longing in your life makes you the most impatient? Why is it so hard to wait?

8. What is the relationship between patience and trusting God and between patience and God's love?

9. Jesus's patience in John 11 led to much suffering. How can suffering, in turn, lead to increased patience? (see Rom. 5:3–4). How have you seen this truth tested or demonstrated in your own experience?

10. In what ways can understanding God's patience toward you help you be more longsuffering toward others?

11. Meditate on John 11:40–44. When you are tempted to be impatient with the delays in your life, how can these verses help you rejoice in God's timing and the glory it brings to him?

CHAPTER 6: LOVE'S FULL EXTENT

Some days it's easy to do kind things for our loved ones. We are overcome with affection for them, and when we have a little time on our hands, we wish to do nice things to show them how much we love them. But other days it's not so easy. We don't want to listen to our loved ones complain about their problems. We are tired, and don't want to do the dishes after dinner. We are hurt, and don't want to reach out and apologize for our part in a disagreement. But it is at these moments that we can show the full extent of our love by taking up a basin and towel to wash their feet, as Jesus did.

1.   Describe a time when you witnessed a surprising and humble act of service, one done for you or for someone else. What effect did that service have on the recipient?

2.   What are some of the situations that provoke you to envy? When are you most tempted to resent someone else's blessing or benefit and secretly resent it or wish to spoil it?

3.   Sometimes our God-given gifts tempt us to boast or be proud. What are some ways we can guard against this temptation?

4.   How are envy, boasting, arrogance, and rudeness related? Why are they antithetical to biblical love?

5.   Read John 13:1–11. What words would you use to describe Jesus's actions here? What is surprising about what he did?

6.   Why didn't Peter want Jesus to wash his feet at first? Why did he later want his head and hands washed as well? Why was it unnecessary, both physically and spiritually, for Jesus to wash Peter's head and hands?

7.   We are told in John 13:11 that Jesus knew Judas would betray him. What does it show about Jesus's love that he washed Judas's feet along with the other disciples'? What does this mean for us?

8.   How did Jesus show the full extent of his love? What characteristics of love as described in 1 Corinthians 13 are exhibited in Jesus's actions in John 13?

9.   This scene takes place shortly before Jesus went to the cross. How does it set the scene for what was to take place there?

10.   How can serving someone else instead of ourselves help us conquer the sins of envy, boasting, arrogance, and rudeness?

11.   Read John 13:12–17. How can you emulate Jesus's example of love poured out? What is one humble act of service that you can do this week? What is one tool of service God has called you to pick up and use on behalf of someone who may not seem to deserve it?

CHAPTER 7: LOVE HOPES

Sometimes in the first blush of romance people see only the good in the person they love. As time goes by, however, reality sets in. We realize that our beloved sometimes gets irritable or hard-headed about things. He or she has annoying habits or disagrees with us on key points. It is then that true love begins to hope and to pray for good things for the beloved. Loving the way Jesus loves means longing for the good of those we love and keeping the faith that they will become more Christlike. It means never giving up hope that, by the power of the Holy Spirit, they can overcome the sins with which they struggle.

1. What is one thing you hope will happen in your life during the coming year? What is one thing you hope will happen in the life of a loved one?

2. Have you ever been tempted to give up hoping for someone because the change you longed to see in him or her seemed impossible? Describe that experience. How does Romans 5:2–5 encourage you to pray for friends and family members without giving up?

3. First Corinthians 13:7 tells us that love hopes all things. What does the word *hope* mean in this definition of love? What kinds of things does true love hope for?

4. How does the love of Jesus inform our love and enable us to hope?

5. Read Hebrews 6:18–19. How is biblical hope different from the world's hope?

6. Read John 17:1–19. What was Jesus hoping for or trusting God to do? How has Jesus's prayer been answered in your life? How have you seen it answered in the church?

7. In what ways is Jesus's love evident in his prayer for his disciples in John 17:6–19?

8. Read John 17:20–26. What does Jesus pray for us? What is the basis for this request?

9. In John 17:20 and 26, what is the mission or end purpose of the unity Jesus wants for us? How does his prayer refocus or redirect your hopes for yourself or your loved ones?

10. In what ways should the example of Jesus's prayer in John 17 influence our own prayers?

11. How can we have a more hopeful love for those around us? What practical things can we do to show them that our love hopes good things for them?

CHAPTER 8: LOVE IS NOT SELF-SEEKING

Children are naturally self-centered. They have to be taught, very gradually, how to share and to think of the needs of others. As adults, it's easy to think we have these lessons figured out. After all, we do kind things for others and try to be considerate of their needs. But how often do we really put ourselves out for others to the point where it infringes on our own needs and desires? And how often do we lay down our lives for a stranger or an enemy?

1. What are some situations at home, at school, at work, or in the church where you can tell that deep down you are more in love with yourself than with others? What circumstances bring out your selfishness rather than self-denial?

2. As you think about the life of Jesus, in what specific ways did he give up his preferences and comfort out of love for others?

3. Our Savior's ultimate selfless act was dying for our sins. Read about his moment of decision in Matthew 26:36–46. What words does the passage use to show how anguished Jesus was? What were some of the reasons for this great anguish? Consider what you may know about Jesus from both inside and outside this passage.

4. What progression do you see in Jesus's prayer between Matthew 26:39 and 42?

5. What principles can we learn about prayer from Matthew 26:36–46?

6. Why is it so hard for us to love others more than ourselves? What are some of the barriers to our loving others in a way that is not self-seeking?

7. How does Jesus's death on the cross relate to our love for others? How can experiencing the love of Jesus help us to love others selflessly?

8. Think about your commitments in the week ahead. How much of your time is already dedicated to yourself—to your own well-being, goals, comfort, and pleasures? How much of your time is set aside for others? Are you satisfied with this balance? If not, what can you do to change it?

9. Consider how you spend your money. Are you stingy or generous when you become aware of people in financial need? Think of the last time that meeting someone else's needs meant that you could not have something you wanted for yourself. What did you do and why?

10. What is one practical way that you can get yourself and your interests out of the way as you seek to love the people God has placed in your path? What is one thing you can do to put someone else first this week?

CHAPTER 9: LOVE BEARS ALL THINGS

To love others is to bear with them, forgiving them for the hurts they inflict upon you both knowingly and unknowingly. Sometimes forbearance requires nothing more than overlooking their rude or inconsiderate behavior. Sometimes the cost is much higher. Paul addressed the full spectrum of sufferings we may be asked to endure at the hands of others by telling us that love bears all things.

1. Chapter 9 offers two possible meanings for "bears all things": to silently bear annoyances and troubles and to conceal and forgive the faults of another rather than exposing them. Describe a time when someone lovingly bore your faults. How did it make you feel? What effect did it have on your relationship?

2. Most likely, 1 Corinthians 13:7 is speaking of love enduring patiently the hurts that are part and parcel of most relationships. What particular insults and hardships do you have to bear from others? What burdens are the hardest for you to bear?

3. Read Matthew 26:45–50, 59–68, and Matthew 27:27–31. What did Jesus endure for us in the final hours before the crucifixion? Make a list of all the sufferings described here—both physical and psychological.

4. In Matthew 26:45–50, 59–68, and Matthew 27:27–31, for what was Jesus mocked?

5. The worst curse that Jesus endured was the cross, perhaps the most painful form of torture ever devised and a shameful way to die (see Deut. 21:22–23). Read Isaiah 53:2–12. What words are used in this passage to describe what Jesus bore for our sins? According to this passage, how did Jesus respond to these insults and sufferings?

6. What good things did Isaiah prophesy would come out of the suffering that Jesus bore on the cross?

7. How can Isaiah 53:2–12 encourage and challenge us as we suffer hurts caused by others?

8. Have you ever thanked Jesus for all the things he bore for you on the cross? Look back at Isaiah 53 and thank him specifically for all the suffering and anguish he endured on your behalf.

9. Sometimes it is not truly loving to bear silently with the faults of others. Some things need to be brought out into the open so they can be dealt with properly, and sometimes we need to protect ourselves from outright abuse. What criteria should we use in trying to decide when to bring the struggles of a loved one before a third party—a pastor, a counselor, or some other person who is involved in the situation?

10. When you are required to bear wounds that seem impossible to endure, what carries you through? On a practical level, what strategies do you employ to help remind you to rely on Jesus?

CHAPTER 10: LOVE TRUSTS

Trust and love are virtually inseparable, because it is nearly impossible to love those we do not trust. The trust we place in people we love is based on what we believe about them. We believe that they won't hurt us, that they will keep their promises to us, and that they will behave according to certain expectations. Ultimately, no one is completely trustworthy except for God. Therefore, he is the only one who totally fulfills the "always believe" characteristic of true love in 1 Corinthians 13:7.

1. Have you ever known someone who trusted God in difficult circumstances? Describe how his or her story influenced you or others to trust in God.

2. Think back on the illustration given of Richard Williams (see pages 147–48), who trusted God all the way to the desperate end of his life. Would you be able to trust God in such circumstances? What is the "what if" that you pray you would be able to trust God through?

3. Read Matthew 27:45–46 and Psalm 22:1–5. What was Jesus saying about his relationship with the Father at that moment? Why is this significant for our salvation?

4. Jesus's final words are found in Luke 23:46. Read that verse along with Psalm 31:1–5, the psalm from which Jesus was quoting. What was Jesus expressing he believed about God the Father and his own suffering? Why is it significant that he ended his earthly life with the words of Luke 23:46 rather than the words of Matthew 27:46?

5. Based on Psalm 31:1–5, what should we believe about the God who loves us?

6. How should our beliefs about the love of God impact our relationships with those around us? How might someone who does not love God love differently from someone who does love God?

7. To be so gullible that we believe only good things about those we love is not truly loving. So what does Paul mean when he tells us that love "always believes"? What kinds of things should we believe about those we love?

8. Charles Spurgeon once said, "I am determined that if all my senses contradict God, I would rather deny every one of them than believe that God could lie." Have your senses ever seemed to contradict God? Would you deny them in favor of believing God? Discuss your answer.

9. In times of suffering, sometimes we find that the biggest difficulty we face is not the circumstances themselves or physical pain but spiritual doubt or depression. Have you ever felt forsaken by God? In those dark times, what did you do to keep the faith?

10. In order to follow Jesus's example of committing your soul to the God who loves you, what things do you need to commit to him in your life right now? Finances? Health? Sinful habits? Family problems? Challenges you face in ministry? Take some time to pray through your present circumstances in a way that demonstrates your trust in God.

CHAPTER 11: LOVE FORGIVES

When we are wronged, sometimes we want to relive the hurt so we can justify our anger. We subconsciously feel that if we let go of our resentment, we are letting the person who hurt us off the hook too easily. So we dwell on our pain and tell others about it so we can have our anger validated. But true love does not keep an account of wrongs. We are to forgive and refuse to harbor ill will toward those who have done us wrong.

1.   When you get really angry with someone, how do you deal with it? Describe a time when you didn't deal with anger well. What were the results of your actions?

2.   When we decide to forgive someone, what actions need to follow our decision in order to carry it out? What practical steps are a necessary part of forgiveness?

3.   The word used for *forgiveness* in 1 Corinthians 13:5 means "to put to one's account." What dimensions does using the language of business add to our common definitions of forgiveness? How does it help us to forgive more fully if we think in terms of a bank account?

4.   Read Matthew 26:30–35, 69–75. What sins was Peter guilty of?

5.   Based on Matthew 26:30–35, 69–75, what words would you use to describe Peter? In what ways do you identify with him?

6.   How have you denied Jesus? Your denial might be a particular incident from your past or daily actions that, if you really think about them, are small ways of denying Christ.

7. Read John 21:1–8. What was Peter's response to Jesus? What emotions can we infer that he was feeling?

8. Read John 21:9–19. How does Jesus show Peter that he is forgiven? List the actions and words of Jesus that would have had special meaning for penitent Peter.

9. What principles can we draw from Jesus's forgiveness and reinstatement of Peter that also apply to the way Jesus treats us? What can we apply from this story to help us rightly forgive others?

10. What are the benefits of forgiveness to the forgiver? What are the negative results of holding on to anger and resentment?

11. Lewis Smedes writes, "Love lets the past die. It moves people to a new beginning without settling the past. Love does not have to clear up all misunderstandings. . . . Love prefers to tuck all the loose ends of past rights and wrongs in the bosom of forgiveness—and pushes us into a new start." Who comes to mind when you read this quote? What steps do you want to take to move closer to truly forgiving him or her?

CHAPTER 12: LOVE NEVER FAILS

If you've ever been let down by someone close to you, you know the importance of promises kept. Whether it is a child whose parent didn't pick her up when promised or a wife abandoned by her spouse, the heart's deepest longing is to be loved by someone who won't betray or disappoint. Earthly love might let us down, but God never will. His love never fails.

1. Surveys on the subject of fears tell us that people's most common fear is public speaking. What is your biggest fear?

2. Describe the time when you first found the love of Christ or a time when your affection for him was especially vibrant. How did you express your love for God at that time?

3. Why will love last longer than other gifts, such as prophecy and tongues?

4. What circumstances make you wonder if God still loves you? What makes you feel separated from his love?

5. Read Romans 8:31–39. According to this passage, how has God shown love to us? List all the things you can find.

6. According to Romans 8:31–39, how can we know that God's love never fails? What things are unable to separate us from his love? What categories of life do these examples cover? For example, "things present" and "things to come" would fit into the category of *time*.

7. What do you do, or could you do, to remind yourself of God's unfailing love at times when you wonder whether God loves you? What practical strategies would help you to trust God during dark and doubtful days?

8. How can we follow Jesus's example of love that never fails? What does this kind of love look like in the main relationships of your life? In the ministry that God has for you?

9. Read 1 Corinthians 14:1. What are some ways that we can pursue love? What attitudes and actions does this command entail?

10. Look back through 1 Corinthians 13. Which characteristic of love do you find the hardest to live out? Which aspect comes most naturally to you? How can you grow in your areas of weakness?

NOTES

CHAPTER 1: NOTHING WITHOUT LOVE

1. *Oxford English Dictionary,* 13th ed., sv "encomium."
2. Gordon D. Fee, *The First Epistle to the Corinthians,* New International Commentary on the New Testament (Grand Rapids, MI: Eerdmans, 1987), 626.
3. Jonathan Edwards, *Charity and Its Fruits* (1852; repr. Edinburgh: Banner of Truth, 2005), 1.
4. Charles Hodge, *An Exposition of the First Epistle to the Corinthians* (repr. London: Banner of Truth, 1958), 264.
5. Anthony C. Thiselton, *The First Epistle to the Corinthians,* New International Greek Testament Commentary (Grand Rapids, MI: Eerdmans, 2000), 1036.
6. W. W. Klein, "Noisy Gong or Acoustic Vase? A Note on 1 Cor. 13:1," *New Testament Studies* 32 (1986): 286–89.
7. J. Moffatt, *The First Epistle of Paul to the Corinthians,* Moffatt New Testament Commentary (London: Hodder & Stoughton, 1938), 192.
8. Josh Moody made this comparison in a sermon at College Church in Wheaton, Illinois, on September 19, 2010.
9. Gennadius of Constantinople, "13:1–3 The Law of Love," quoted in *1–2 Corinthians,* Ancient Christian Commentary on Scripture, NT 7, ed. Gerald Bray (Downers Grove, IL: InterVarsity, 1999), 131.
10. Thiselton, *First Epistle to the Corinthians,* 1041.
11. Edwards, *Charity,* 57.
12. Another fresh insight from Josh Moody's preaching on this passage.

CHAPTER 2: LOVE THAT IS BETTER THAN LIFE

1. As recounted in Melissa Howard, "Understanding 'More Love to Thee, O Christ'," http://christianmusic.suite101.com/article.cfm/understanding_more_love_to_thee_o_christ (accessed 9/7/2009).
2. Elizabeth Payson Prentiss, quoted in William J. and Ardythe Peterson, *The Complete Book of Hymns: Inspiring Stories about 600 Hymns and Praise Songs* (Carol Stream, IL: Tyndale, 2006), 349.
3. Elizabeth Payson Prentiss, quoted in Robert J. Morgan, *Then Sings My Soul: 150 of the World's Greatest Hymn Stories* (Nashville, TN: Thomas Nelson, 2003), 133.
4. John Chrysostom, "Homilies on the Epistles of Paul to the Corinthians," 32.6, quoted in *1–2 Corinthians,* Ancient Christian Commentary on Scripture, NT 7, ed. Gerald Bray (Downers Grove, IL: InterVarsity, 1999), 131.
5. Ibid., 131.
6. C. S. Lewis, *The Four Loves* (New York: Harcourt Brace Jovanovich, 1960), 11.
7. Anthony C. Thiselton, *The First Epistle to the Corinthians,* New International Greek Testament Commentary (Grand Rapids, MI: Eerdmans, 2000), 1047.
8. Henry Drummond, *The Greatest Thing in the World* (New York: Grosset & Dunlap, n.d.), 28.
9. Ceslaus Spicq, *Theological Lexicon of the New Testament,* trans. and ed. J. D. Ernest, 3 vols. (Peabody, MA: Hendrickson, 1994), s.v. "agape."
10. Ceslaus Spicq, *Agape dans le Nouveau Testament* (Paris: Etudes, Bibliques, 1959), 2:151.
11. Gordon D. Fee, *The First Epistle to the Corinthians,* New International Commentary on the New Testament (Grand Rapids, MI: Eerdmans, 1987), 636.
12. See Charles Hodge, *An Exposition of the First Epistle to the Corinthians* (repr. London: Banner of Truth, 1958), 269; Jonathan Edwards, *Charity and Its Fruits* (1852; repr. Edinburgh: Banner of Truth, 2005), 96.

13. Lewis B. Smedes, *Love within Limits: A Realist's View of 1 Corinthians 13* (Grand Rapids, MI: Eerdmans, 1978), 15.

14. John Chrysostom, *Homilies on the Epistles of First Corinthians*, trans. Talbot W. Chambers, ed. Philip Schaff, Nicene and Post-Nicene Fathers, First Series (1889; repr. Peabody, MA: Hendrickson, 1994), 10:195.

15. Leo Tolstoy, as summarized by Alan Paton in *A Journey Continued: An Autobiography* (New York: Collier, 1988), 285.

16. Henry Boardman, *A Handful of Corn* (New York: Anson D. F. Randolph, 1884), 137.

17. Paul E. Miller, *Love Walked Among Us: Learning to Love Like Jesus* (Colorado Springs, CO: NavPress, 2001), 164.

18. Smedes, *Love within Limits*, 12.

19. Lewis, *Four Loves*, 177.

20. Amy Carmichael, *If* (London: SPCK, 1938), 9.

21. Edwards, *Charity*, 97.

22. Tertullian, *Apology* (3:39), quoted in David E. Garland, *First Corinthians*, Baker Exegetical Commentary on the New Testament (Grand Rapids, MI: Baker, 2003), 617.

CHAPTER 3: LOVE IS NOT IRRITABLE

1. James Hope Moulton and George Milligan, *The Vocabulary of the Greek Testament: Illustrated from the Papyri and Other Non-Literary Sources* (Grand Rapids, MI: Eerdmans, 1963), 496.

2. Charles Hodge, *An Exposition of the First Epistle to the Corinthians* (repr. London: Banner of Truth, 1958), 270.

3. Anthony C. Thiselton, *The First Epistle to the Corinthians*, New International Greek Testament Commentary (Grand Rapids, MI: Eerdmans, 2000), 1052.

4. David E. Garland, *First Corinthians*, Baker Exegetical Commentary on the New Testament (Grand Rapids, MI: Baker, 2003), 618.

5. Lewis B. Smedes, *Love within Limits: A Realist's View of 1 Corinthians 13* (Grand Rapids, MI: Eerdmans, 1978), 60.

6. Jonathan Edwards, *Charity and Its Fruits* (1852; repr. Edinburgh: Banner of Truth, 2005), 196.

7. Smedes, *Love within Limits*, 58.

8. This story is told by Brad S. Gregory in "Saints' Lives Decoded?" *Books and Culture* (July/August 2009): 12.

9. Henry Drummond, *The Greatest Thing in the World* (New York: Grosset & Dunlap, n.d.), 24.

10. C. S. Lewis, *The Four Loves* (London: Geoffrey Bles, 1961), 154.

CHAPTER 4: LOVE'S HOLY JOY

1. Jonathan Edwards, *Charity and Its Fruits* (1852; repr. Edinburgh: Banner of Truth, 2005), 221.

2. Gordon D. Fee, *The First Epistle to the Corinthians*, New International Commentary on the New Testament (Grand Rapids, MI: Eerdmans, 1987), 639.

3. Edwards, *Charity*, 222.

4. Anthony C. Thiselton, *The First Epistle to the Corinthians*, New International Greek Testament Commentary (Grand Rapids, MI: Eerdmans, 2000), 1054.

5. Henry Drummond, *The Greatest Thing in the World* (New York: Grosset & Dunlap, n.d.), 27.

6. E.g., Fee, *First Epistle*, 639.

7. See Paul Miller, *Love Walked Among Us: Learning to Love Like Jesus* (Colorado Springs, CO: NavPress, 2001), 51.

8. Ibid., 52–53.

CHAPTER 5: LOVE WAITS

1. This story comes from the family of Kimberly Wynne, whose husband, Carroll, was a longtime colleague in ministry at Philadelphia's Tenth Presbyterian Church.

2. Charles Hodge, *An Exposition of the First Epistle to the Corinthians* (repr. London: Banner of Truth, 1958), 269.

3. Leon Morris, *The First Epistle of Paul to the Corinthians*, Tyndale New Testament Commentaries (Grand Rapids, MI: Eerdmans, 1958), 184.

4. Anthony C. Thiselton, *The First Epistle to the Corinthians*, New International Greek Testament Commentary (Grand Rapids, MI: Eerdmans, 2000), 1046.

5. John W. Sanderson, *The Fruit of the Spirit* (1972; repr. Phillipsburg, NJ: Presbyterian & Reformed, 1985), 88.

6. James Montgomery Boice, *The Gospel of John, Vol. 3: Those Who Received Him, John 9–12* (Grand Rapids, MI: Baker, 1999), 826.

7. Jonathan Edwards, *Charity and Its Fruits* (1852; repr. Edinburgh: Banner of Truth, 2005), 79–80.

8. Sanderson, *Fruit of the Spirit*, 88.

9. Boice, *Gospel of John*, 826.

10. James Montgomery Boice makes a similar point in his commentary on John (p. 828).

11. Alexander Maclaren, *Expositions of Holy Scripture, Vol. 7: St. John, Chapters 9–14* (Grand Rapids, MI: Eerdmans, 1959), 78.

CHAPTER 6: LOVE'S FULL EXTENT

1. I owe this insight to Jonathan Edwards, *Charity and Its Fruits* (1852; repr. Edinburgh: Banner of Truth, 2005), 111. In his comments on 1 Corinthians 13:4, Edwards distinguishes between our response to "the good possessed by others" and to "the good possessed by ourselves."

2. Anthony C. Thiselton, *The First Epistle to the Corinthians*, New International Greek Testament Commentary (Grand Rapids, MI: Eerdmans, 2000), 1048.

3. Cornelius Plantinga Jr., *Not the Way It's Supposed to Be: A Breviary of Sin* (Grand Rapids, MI: Eerdmans, 1995), 169.

4. Edwards, *Charity*, 112.

5. Ibid., 113.

6. Thiselton, *First Epistle*, 1048.

7. Lewis B. Smedes, *Love within Limits: A Realist's View of 1 Corinthians 13* (Grand Rapids, MI: Eerdmans, 1978), 28; emphasis original.

8. Thiselton, *First Epistle*, 1048.

9. Smedes, *Love within Limits*, 33.

10. James Montgomery Boice, *The Gospel of John, Vol. 4: Peace in Storm, John 13–17* (Grand Rapids, MI: Baker, 1999), 999.

11. Ibid., 1011.

12. Ibid.

13. "Love on Its Knees" is the title James Boice gives to one of his expositions of John 13:2–15. Ibid., 1007.

14. Donald English, *The Message of Mark: The Mystery of Faith* (Downers Grove, IL: InterVarsity, 1992), 182.

CHAPTER 7: LOVE HOPES

1. James R. Edwards recounts these events in "The One Time the Church Was One," *The Edwards Epistle*, vol. 18 (Summer 2009): 1–2.

2. Richard B. Hays, *First Corinthians*, Interpretation (Louisville, KY: John Knox, 1997), 228.

3. Gordon D. Fee, *The First Epistle to the Corinthians*, New International Commentary on the New Testament (Grand Rapids, MI: Eerdmans, 1987), 640.

4. Anthony C. Thiselton, *The First Epistle to the Corinthians*, New International Greek Testament Commentary (Grand Rapids, MI: Eerdmans, 2000), 1057.

5. David E. Garland, *First Corinthians*, Baker Exegetical Commentary on the New Testament (Grand Rapids, MI: Baker, 2003), 619.

6. John Chrysostom, *Homilies on the Epistles of First Corinthians*, trans. Talbot W. Chambers, ed. Philip Schaff, Nicene and Post-Nicene Fathers, First Series (1889; repr. Peabody, MA: Hendrickson, 1994), 198.

7. Jonathan Edwards, *Charity and Its Fruits* (1852; repr. Edinburgh: Banner of Truth, 2005), 271.

8. Henry Drummond, *The Greatest Thing in the World* (New York: Grosset & Dunlap, n.d.), 32.

9. Lewis B. Smedes, *Love within Limits: A Realist's View of 1 Corinthians 13* (Grand Rapids, MI: Eerdmans, 1978), 103.

CHAPTER 8: LOVE IS NOT SELF-SEEKING

1. Jonathan Edwards, *Charity and Its Fruits* (1852; repr. Edinburgh: Banner of Truth, 2005), 157.

2. Ibid., 172.

3. David E. Garland, *First Corinthians*, Baker Exegetical Commentary on the New Testament (Grand Rapids, MI: Baker, 2003), 616.

4. Gordon D. Fee, *The First Epistle to the Corinthians*, New International Commentary on the New Testament (Grand Rapids, MI: Eerdmans, 1987), 638.

5. Erich Fromm, quoted in Lewis B. Smedes, *Love within Limits: A Realist's View of 1 Corinthians 13* (Grand Rapids, MI: Eerdmans, 1978), 46.

6. Shirley MacLaine's 1977 *Washington Post* interview, as quoted by Charles R. Swindoll in *Growing Deep in the Christian Life: Essential Truths for Becoming Strong in the Faith* (Grand Rapids, MI: Zondervan, 1995), 89.

7. C. S. Lewis, *The Four Loves* (New York: Harcourt, Brace, Jovanovich, 1960), 177.

8. Richard Baxter, quoted in J. C. Ryle, *Expository Thoughts on the Gospels, Luke* (1858; repr. Cambridge: James Clarke, 1976), 2:427.

9. Benjamin Breckinridge Warfield, "The Emotional Life of Our Lord," in *The Person and Work of Christ*, ed. Samuel G. Craig (Philadelphia: Presbyterian and Reformed, 1950), 132–33.

10. Quoted in John Calvin, *Original Sin: A Cultural History*, ed. Alan Jacobs (New York: HarperCollins, 2008), 170–71.

11. Quoted in Lewis, *Four Loves*, 163.

12. Amy Carmichael, *If* (London: SPCK, 1938), 82.

13. Fee, *The First Epistle*, 631.

14. See Christian Smith, Michael O. Emerson, and Patricia Snell, *Passing the Plate: Why American Christians Don't Give Away More Money* (Oxford: Oxford University Press, 2008).

15. Edwards, *Charity*, 171.

16. The story behind "Have Thine Own Way" is recounted in "Sarah Pollard Didn't Like Her Name," *Glimpses of Christian History*, as accessed on November 9, 2009, on http://www.christianity.com/ChurchHistory/11630530.

CHAPTER 9: LOVE BEARS ALL THINGS

1. Richard Wurmbrand, *Tortured for Christ* (1967; repr. Glendale, CA: Diane Books, 1976), 58.

2. Ibid., 57.

3. Charles Hodge, *An Exposition of the First Epistle to the Corinthians* (repr. London: Banner of Truth, 1958), 271; emphasis in original.

4. Lewis B. Smedes, *Love within Limits: A Realist's View of 1 Corinthians 13* (Grand Rapids, MI: Eerdmans, 1978), 86.

5. H. A. W. Meyer, quoted in Anthony C. Thiselton, *The First Epistle to the Corinthians*, New International Greek Testament Commentary (Grand Rapids, MI: Eerdmans, 2000), 1058.

6. Jonathan Edwards, *Charity and Its Fruits* (1852; repr. Edinburgh: Banner of Truth, 2005), 251.

7. Hodge, *Exposition*, 271.

8. Ibid.

9. Leon Morris, *The First Epistle of Paul to the Corinthians*, Tyndale New Testament Commentaries (Grand Rapids, MI: Eerdmans, 1958), 186.

10. Smedes, *Love within Limits*, 112.

11. Edwards, *Charity*, 286.

12. Josh Moody made this point in a sermon he preached at College Church, Wheaton, Illinois, September 19, 2010.

13. John Chrysostom, "Homilies on the Epistles of Paul to the Corinthians," 32.6, quoted in *1–2 Corinthians*, Ancient Christian Commentary on Scripture, ed. Gerald Bray, NT 7 (Downers Grove, IL: InterVarsity, 2003), 133.

14. James Montgomery Boice, *The Gospel of Matthew, vol. 2: The Triumph of the King, Matthew 18–28* (Grand Rapids, MI: Baker, 2001), 610.

15. This spiritual is quoted by John Lovell Jr. in *Black Song: The Forge and the Flame* (New York: Paragon, 1972), 467.

16. Corrie ten Boom, with John and Elizabeth Sherrill, *The Hiding Place* (Washington Depot, CT: Chosen, 1971), 178–79.

CHAPTER 10: LOVE TRUSTS

1. Ian MacPherson, *The Punctuality of God* (Manchester: Puritan Press, 1946), quoted at http://www.christianity.co.nz/life_death9.htm.

2. Leon Morris, *The First Epistle of Paul to the Corinthians*, Tyndale New Testament Commentaries (Grand Rapids, MI: Eerdmans, 1958), 185.

3. Lewis B. Smedes, *Love within Limits: A Realist's View of 1 Corinthians 13* (Grand Rapids, MI: Eerdmans, 1978), 99.

4. David E. Garland, *First Corinthians*, Baker Exegetical Commentary on the New Testament (Grand Rapids, MI: Baker, 2003), 619.

5. Gordon D. Fee, *The First Epistle to the Corinthians*, New International Commentary on the New Testament (Grand Rapids, MI: Eerdmans, 1987), 640.

6. Anthony C. Thiselton, *The First Epistle to the Corinthians*, New International Greek Testament Commentary (Grand Rapids, MI: Eerdmans, 2000), 1057.

7. Smedes, *Love within Limits*, 96.

8. These examples are recounted by James Montgomery Boice in *The Heart of the Cross* (Wheaton, IL: Crossway, 1999).

9. http://www.christianity.com/ChurchHistory/11629983/.

10. Alan Paton, *Journey Continued: An Autobiography* (New York: Collier, 1988), 275.

CHAPTER 11: LOVE FORGIVES

1. Visit http://www.amenclinic.com, "Brain Disorder Research."

2. The scientific research on emotional black holes is briefly summarized in Tom White, "Holes in Your Head—or Helmet of Salvation?" *Voice of the Martyrs* (September, 2008): 2.

3. Jonathan Edwards, *Charity and Its Fruits* (1852; repr. Edinburgh: Banner of Truth, 2005), 204.

4. David E. Garland, *First Corinthians*, Baker Exegetical Commentary on the New Testament (Grand Rapids, MI: Baker, 2003), 618.

5. Brian J. Dodd, *Praying Jesus' Way: A Guide for Beginners and Veterans* (Downers Grove, IL: InterVarsity, 1997), 101.

6. Eric E. Wright, *Revolutionary Forgiveness* (Auburn, MA: Evangelical Press, 2002), 147.

7. Lewis B. Smedes, *Love within Limits: A Realist's View of 1 Corinthians 13* (Grand Rapids, MI: Eerdmans, 1978), 67.

8. Ibid., 67.

9. Garland, *First Corinthians*, 619.

10. Smedes, *Love within Limits*, 71.

11. Gordon D. Fee, *The First Epistle to the Corinthians*, New International Commentary on the New Testament (Grand Rapids, MI: Eerdmans, 1987), 631.

12. Amy Carmichael, *If* (London: SPCK, 1938) 4, 11, 19, 36, 40.

13. John Newton, quoted in Steve Turner, *Amazing Grace: The Story of America's Most Beloved Song* (New York: HarperCollins, 2002), 110.

14. Kim Phuc, "The Long Road to Forgiveness," with Anne Penman, Canadian Broadcasting Corporation (June 30, 2008).

CHAPTER 12: LOVE NEVER FAILS

1. Augustine, *The Confessions of St. Augustine*, trans. Rex Warner, New American Library (New York: Penguin, 1963), 235.

2. Ibid.

3. David E. Garland, *First Corinthians*, Baker Exegetical Commentary on the New Testament (Grand Rapids, MI: Baker, 2003), 621.

4. Gordon D. Fee, *The First Epistle to the Corinthians*, New International Commentary on the New Testament (Grand Rapids, MI: Eerdmans, 1987), 642.

5. Ibid., 647–48.

6. Mark Dever, *Twelve Challenges Churches Face* (Wheaton, IL: Crossway, 2008), 152.

7. Jonathan Edwards, *Charity and Its Fruits* (1852; repr. Edinburgh: Banner of Truth, 2005), 315.

8. Henry Drummond, *The Greatest Thing in the World* (New York: James Pott, 1874).

9. Charles Hodge, *An Exposition of the First Epistle to the Corinthians* (repr. London: Banner of Truth, 1958), 271.

10. Caspar Olevianus, quoted in John Willison, *The Practical Works of John Willison*, ed. W. M. Hetherington (Glasgow, 1852), 322.

11. Alexander Maclaren, *Expositions of Holy Scripture*, vol. 8 (Grand Rapids, MI: Eerdmans, 1959), 213.

12. This story has been variously attributed to A. W. Tozer and Warren Candler.

13. James Montgomery Boice, *Romans: The Reign of Grace, Romans 5:1–8:39* (Grand Rapids, MI: Baker, 1993), 2:983.

14. Robert Bruce, quoted by D. C. MacNichol in *Robert Bruce: Minister in the Kirk of Edinburgh* (Edinburgh: Oliphant, Anderson & Ferrier, 1907).

15. Edwards, *Charity*, 24.

GENERAL INDEX

SCRIPTURE INDEX

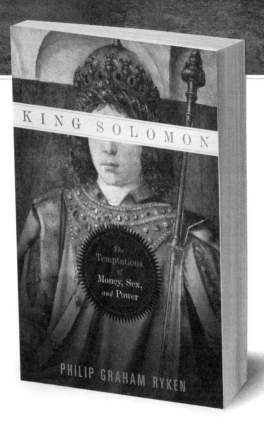

LIVING IN THE LOVE OF THE THREE-IN-ONE

Relating to God as Father, Son, and Holy Spirit can have a deep impact on one's faith. Philip Ryken and Michael LeFebvre outline the saving, mysterious, practical, and glorious Trinity in this theologically rich resource.